NETHERLANDS

Amsterdam

ent

Brussels

BELGIUM

Namur

Cologne

ims

Rhine

Meuse

Moselle

Boppard

Ebern

GERMANY

Nuremberg

Heilbronn

Burg Weiler

Pont-Saint-Vincent

Lichtenthal

Ingolstadt

oyes

Strasbourg

Froville

Sulz am Neckar

Vienna

outiers-Saint-Jean

Freiburg

Salzburg

Ebreichsdorf

Dijon

AUSTRIA

Beaune

un

Innsbruck

Maria-Strassengel

Poligny

SWITZERLAND

ny

ITTA

Quattro Castella

ignon

s

Lucca

Florence

Terranuova

Siena

Tiber

Monticchio

Fiano Romano

Rome

THE CLOISTERS

The Metropolitan Museum of Art

THE CLOISTERS

The Building and the Collection of

Medieval Art in Fort Tryon Park

BY JAMES J. RORIMER

Third Edition, revised in collaboration with

Margaret B. Freeman and the Staff of the

Medieval Department and The Cloisters

New York, 1963

FRONTISPIECE: *The Cloisters, seen from the south*

Photography by William F. Pons, Thomas McAdams, Edward Milla, and L. F. Kenett. Designed by Peter Oldenburg. Composed in English Monotype Bembo by Clarke & Way, Inc., and printed on Stevens-Nelson Text by The Meriden Gravure Company. Endpaper map designed by Elmer Smith and printed on Hamilton Kilmory Cover by The Meriden Gravure Company. Cover plates for the paperbound edition engraved by V. Siviter Smith & Co., Ltd. and printed on S. D. Warren's Cumberland Gloss Cover by Clarke & Way, Inc. Clothbound edition bound by Russell-Rutter Company; paperbound edition bound by Clarke & Way, Inc.; binding die design by Fritz Kredel.

PREFACE TO
THE FIRST EDITION

IN 1925 John D. Rockefeller, Jr., presented to The Metropolitan Museum of Art a sum of money with which to purchase and maintain the collection of medieval sculpture and architectural material assembled by George Grey Barnard and since 1914 open to the public in a brick structure built especially for it on Fort Washington Avenue.

The Barnard collection was perhaps the most extensive of its kind in America at that time. Both the way in which it was brought together and the manner in which it was displayed were remarkable achievements of enthusiasm and industry on the part of a single individual. Large sections of the cloisters of the long abandoned and ruined monasteries of Saint-Michel-de-Cuxa, Saint-Guilhem-le-Désert, Bonnefont-en-Comminges, and Trie formed the nucleus of a collection which there had been brought together such notable pieces of medieval sculpture as the tomb effigy of Jean d'Alluye, a Romanesque torso of the crucified Christ, wooden figures of Mary and John from a thirteenth century Crucifixion group, and numerous statues of the Virgin from the Île-de-France and Lorraine.

When in 1926 the collection was rearranged and the building reopened as a branch of the Metropolitan Museum and called The Cloisters, Mr. and Mrs. Rockefeller added some forty more sculptures from their private collection, and two years later Mr. Rockefeller presented the great tomb of Count Armengol VII.

From time to time, during the succeeding ten years, Mr. Rocke-feller has given other important medieval monuments to the collection, but for the exhibition of most of these additional gifts the original structure was wholly inadequate. Therefore, when in June 1930, he presented to the City the high land overlooking the Hudson which is now Fort Tryon Park, he reserved the northern hilltop for a new and larger Cloisters museum, the design of which he entrusted to Charles Collens of the firm of Allen, Collens and Willis of Boston. In planning the installation of the objects in the old Cloisters which were to be shown with the later acquisitions in the new, Joseph Breck, Assistant Director of the Metropolitan Museum, worked in collaboration with Mr. Collens. Upon Mr. Breck's death in 1933 this responsibility fell to James J. Rorimer, who had been closely associated with him in the Museum since 1927 and who became Curator of the Department of Medieval Art on January 1, 1934, and of The Cloisters on January 1, 1938. Throughout the period of actual construction, which began in 1934, Mr. Collens and Mr. Rorimer have been in intimate co-operation, and to these two more than to anyone else the present form of The Cloisters is due. The Committee on the Buildings, under the chairmanship of William Church Osborn, has had general oversight of the undertaking for the Trustees, and Mr. Rockefeller has followed every detail with the deepest interest.

The objects presented during the last ten years by Mr. Rocke-feller are now shown for the first time in the new Cloisters and add immeasurably to the interest of the collection. To select but a few, there are the Spanish thirteenth century Adoration group from Cerezo de Riotirón and the frescoes from the chapter house of the monastery of San Pedro de Arlanza; the chapter house from the doorway from the thirteenth century French abbey at Moutiers-Saint-Jean; and a magnificent fourteenth century statue of the Virgin and Child from the Île-de-France. But of all the great works of art now in The Cloisters, perhaps precedence should be given to the famous fifteenth century French or Flemish tapestries depicting The Hunt of the Unicorn—the outstanding set of Gothic tapestries in this country.

To the original Cloisters collection and to the incomparable additions made to it by Mr. Rockefeller, further additions have come as gifts from other friends of the Museum and through purchase. George Blumenthal has presented ten twelfth century corbels, a twelfth century doorway from Reugny, four fifteenth century windows from Sens, and a contemporary arcade from the priory at Froville. Stephen C. Clark presented three of the capitals from Trie. With income from the Rogers Fund the Museum has purchased parts of the choir of the twelfth century church at Langon now installed in the Romanesque Chapel.

From the collections in the main building of the Metropolitan Museum there have been moved to The Cloisters a number of objects, of which perhaps the most notable are the twelfth century Spanish crucifix, the thirteenth century lion from Zamora and portal from Frías, and the fifteenth century ceiling from Illescas.

May, 1938   H. E. WINLOCK

PREFACE TO
THE THIRD EDITION

THIS book was first published in 1938 and has since undergone numerous reprintings, usually with slight alterations to incorporate changes and additions at The Cloisters. By 1951 the number and importance of these additions, such as the Chalice of Antioch, the Catalan tombs of the Counts of Urgel, and the Nine Heroes tapestries and other pieces purchased from the Joseph Brummer estate, made necessary an extensively revised and enlarged edition.

In 1952 the continuing growth of the collections at The Cloisters was assured with a large fund established by John D. Rockefeller, Jr. This fund has made possible the purchase of such diverse objects as the Campin altarpiece, two rare French Books of Hours, and the Saint Stephen reliquary, and enabled the Museum to bring the Fuentidueña apse to America. In the past ten years over five hundred works of medieval art have been secured, including ten paintings, twelve tapestries and rugs, more than eighty sculptures, 204 pieces of ironwork from the Samuel B. Yellin collection, and 86 examples of Hispano-Moresque ceramics from the William Randolph Hearst collection.

Several welcome gifts have enriched The Cloisters in recent years, including doorways and other architectural stonework given by The Hearst Foundation, a fifteenth century tapestry of the Life of the Virgin donated by Charles F. Iklé, a major portion of the recently acquired frescoes from San Baudelio de Berlanga given by The Clowes Fund, Inc. and E. B. Martindale, and two fourteenth century Sienese paintings as a bequest of John D. Rockefeller, Jr. These additions have required yet another revised and enlarged edition of this guide in order to give a comprehensive description of the collections.

Margaret B. Freeman, Curator of The Cloisters since 1955, and Thomas P. F. Hoving, Assistant Curator, have made notable changes and additions in this new edition of the guide. Also among the many who have given valued assistance during its preparation are the following members of the staff of the Department of Medieval Art and The Cloisters: William H. Forsyth, Associate Curator of Medieval Art; Vera K. Ostoia, Research Associate; Carmen Gómez-Moreno, Assistant Curator; Edward P. Lawson, Assistant Curator; and Bonnie Young, Staff Lecturer.

1962   JAMES J. RORIMER
                                                                    Director

CONTENTS

INTRODUCTION

THE purpose of The Cloisters, as expressed by the donor, John D. Rockefeller, Jr., is to provide a culminating point of interest in the architectural design of Fort Tryon Park and to display in an appropriate setting works of art and architecture of the Middle Ages. The original plan of the museum was developed around elements of the cloisters of five French monasteries, dating from the twelfth to the fifteenth century; it was from these elements that the name of The Cloisters was derived.

The Middle Ages embraced the long moment of Christian history from the time of Constantine, the first Christian emperor (311–337), to the beginning of the Renaissance, which began in Italy in the fifteenth century, but as late as the sixteenth century in the countries of northern Europe. Both the buildings and the works of art displayed at The Cloisters represent various artistic styles of two periods of the Middle Ages: the Romanesque and the Gothic.

The Romanesque era comes well along in this lengthy span of history; the style flourished in the eleventh and twelfth centuries. Its primary characteristics in architecture are the round arch and walls built thick to support barrel vaults, reminiscent of the structures of ancient Rome. But the period is also noted for the reappearance of monumental figure sculpture and for the achievement of an indissoluble unity of sculpture with architecture.

In the Romanesque period a profusion of figures began to be carved in stone in many cathedrals, churches, and monasteries. Episodes from the Old and New Testaments and the Apocryphal Gospels, and stories from the lives of saints began to cover the façades of churches, their pilasters, archivolts, and tympana, and the

capitals of columns in cloisters. The entire fabric of church buildings proclaimed the teaching of the faith, for didacticism was the
principal intent. But at the same time neither artists nor patrons
had lost their taste for pure ornament. Thus, along with biblical
narrative appeared brilliant decoration abstracted from the forms
of plants and trees and animals. Some of the myriad creatures that
populate Romanesque churches and paintings are based on real
animals; others are the successful results of vivid artistic imagina-
tion.

The Romanesque style is strong, at times severe, in its monumentality and abstraction. It is bold and summary in the delineation
of overall form, intricate and energetic in details. It spread in waves
throughout Europe, along roads that led from greater to smaller
pilgrimage shrines and monasteries, and thus became international.
It reached its culmination around the middle of the twelfth century.

By this time a new style of architecture had begun in France. Its
cradle was the Île-de-France, and its chief progenitor the gifted
Abbot Suger of Saint-Denis, minister to Louis VI (reigned 1108–
1137) and regent while Louis VII (reigned 1137–1180) was absent
on the Second Crusade. Unlike the Romanesque, with its heavy
walls and closed dark interiors, the Gothic building, with its
pointed arches and the complicated system of thrust and counter-
thrust that support its vaulting, gives the effect of an open framework, illuminated by great windows filled with glass stained the
colors of jewels. Both eye and spirit are led outward toward the
brilliant windows and upward to the soaring vaults with their
intricate ribs.

The Romanesque church is solid, enduring, austere; the Gothic,
infinitely rich in decoration, constructed and carved in multi-
tudinous facets, gives simultaneous impressions of the monumental and the weightless. In this period sculpture and ornament
began to free themselves from the confines of architectural form.

Figures on façades, doorways, capitals began to move upward and outward, away from the surface.

The thirteenth century is called the high Gothic period, the period that combined the austerity of the late Romanesque and the transcendental mysticism of the Gothic. The fourteenth century saw an increasing desire for elegance, sophistication, and the mundane, which reached its climax in the late Gothic of the fifteenth century.

Of the great cathedral building of the Middle Ages, The Cloisters gives but a suggestion; it is patterned on that more private manifestation of the Church, the monastery.

Monasticism, the gathering together of a community of members devoted to a religious ideal, was known long before Christian times, but the urge, inherent in the Christian faith, toward asceticism and withdrawal from the material world offered powerful stimuli for its practice. Christian monasticism is of two fundamental types, the Antonian and the Benedictine. The former, eremitical and individualistic, takes its name from Saint Anthony (about 250–about 355), who retired into the desert and devoted himself to religious exercises. Benedictine monasticism, which was to have a much greater influence than Antonian on Western Christendom, was initiated by Saint Benedict of Nursia (about 480–543). Its emphasis was upon the cenobium, the community, and its rule required that each member of the group engage in some active and constructive work. Saint Benedict founded fourteen monasteries, of which the most famous was at Monte Cassino, established about 520.

The foundation of the Benedictine abbey of Cluny in 910 marked the establishment of the most important of the great monastic orders that became so influential in the Middle Ages and that were largely responsible for the building of churches. It was the object of the Cluniac order to ensure uniform observance of the Rule of Saint Benedict by setting up a centralized organization for the government of monasteries. At the height of its power in the twelfth century the order controlled more than three hundred monasteries in France, Italy, Germany, and Spain.

From about 1125 to 1225 the Cistercian order, founded at the abbey of Cîteaux in 1098, established reforms and assumed leadership of European monasticism; its intention was to follow strictly and literally the Rule of Saint Benedict. Saint Bernard (1090–1153), abbot of the famous Cistercian abbey of Clairvaux, did much through his writings and teachings to reform monastic life. The Cistercians granted dependent monasteries greater freedom in the management of their own affairs than the Cluniac order, but required the abbots to assemble once a year at Clairvaux. In art the Cistercians forbade the depiction of figures and reduced ornament to the simplest types.

There were numerous other orders—for example, the Camaldolese and the Vallombrosans in Italy and the Carthusians in France— but these were contemplative, tending toward the Antonian rather than the Benedictine ideal. Toward the end of the thirteenth century monasticism declined, and by the time of the Reformation the institution had already lost much of its great power.

In all western European monasteries the most important buildings were grouped around a central cloister, an open court with a covered and arcaded passageway along the sides. The different buildings of the monastery and their disposition followed the requirements of monastic life. The oldest existing plan of a monastery, drawn on parchment about 830, is preserved at the abbey of Saint-Gall in Switzerland. The buildings are represented in great detail, and many of their features are typical of monasteries built in the ensuing centuries. In order to illustrate the principal characteristics of medieval monasteries and to make clear the role and original arrangement of the parts of ancient monastic buildings preserved in The Cloisters, the plan of the abbey of Royaumont is reproduced on the following page.

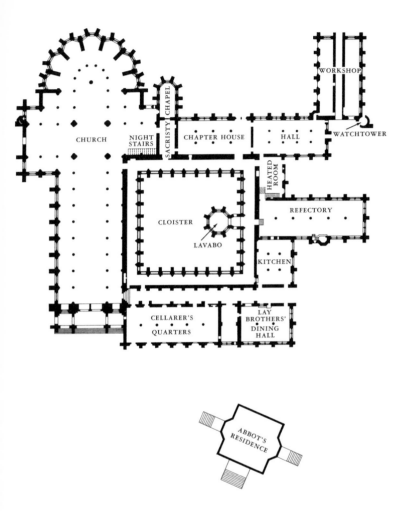

Most of the monks' activities, other than those of worship, centered in the cloister. It was there that they walked in meditation and on occasion were permitted to talk informally. (Formal discussions took place in the chapter house.) In the cloister they had their school, studied, and copied manuscripts. The cloisters of western

European monasteries were approximately rectangular in shape. They were placed at one side of the church, preferably the south, and usually in the angle formed by the transept and the nave. One of the walks of the cloister was next to the wall of the nave. The chief building on the opposite walk, facing the church, was the refectory. The chapter house and sometimes the sacristy and the armarium (library) adjoined the transept. The cloister side of the chapter house was almost always open, as at Pontaut (see page 10), although occasionally in northern countries, owing to the cold, it was enclosed. The dormitory was on a second floor, preferably over the chapter house so that the monks could readily reach the church by the night stairs. On the fourth side there were store-rooms (the cellarer's quarters) and workshops. Some very large monasteries, for instance, the great Cistercian abbey of Clairvaux, had several cloisters, as numerous buildings were necessary to serve the complex requirements of a large community.

The Cloisters is not copied from any single medieval building, nor is it a composite of various buildings. The plan, as we have seen, was developed around architectural elements, dating from the twelfth to the fifteenth century, from the cloisters of five French monasteries: Saint-Guilhem-le-Désert, Saint-Michel-de-Cuxa, Bonnefont-en-Comminges, Trie, and Froville (see endpaper map). As the reconstructed cloister from the abbey of Cuxa was to be the central and largest section of the museum, it seemed appropriate to employ in the design of the high tower some of the features of one still standing at Cuxa, one of two which were formerly part of the abbey. The Gothic chapel at the southwest of the building was modeled after thirteenth century chapels at Carcassonne and Monsempron.

Numerous other Romanesque and Gothic architectural elements have been incorporated functionally into the building, in-cluding the Spanish Romanesque apse from Fuentidueña, the chapter house from Pontaut, the stonework from the choir of the church at Langon, some thirty doorways and windows, and stained glass. Care has been exercised to arrange antique objects with relation to their original use. Extensive restoration of the works of art has been avoided.

Prominence has been given the exhibits by making the modern architectural setting unobtrusive. Though the backgrounds are medieval in style, the simplest precedents have been followed. Building materials have been kept subdued along with the architectural design. Millstone granite, quarried and cut by hand near New London, has been used for most of the exterior of the building. Its warm tones recall stone found in southern France, and it is more durable and therefore more suitable for a large modern structure in New York than the stone commonly used for medieval buildings. To give proper scale to the walls, the dimensions of the individual blocks were patterned after those of Romanesque buildings, in particular the church at Corneille-de-Conflent, a few miles from Cuxa. For the interior stonework the principal material is Doria limestone, quarried near Genoa in Italy. When sand-sawn and left without further tooling it has the appearance of weathered stone and harmonizes well with the antique elements in the collection. Color, which was profuse on architecture as well as sculpture during the Middle Ages, has been used sparingly for decoration. To have reproduced the ancient effects would have broken the rule against excessive restoration.

Red roof and floor tiles, copied from examples excavated at Saint-Michel-de-Cuxa, give an effect like that of buildings in southern Europe; and here and there old materials, including beams for the ceiling, planks for the doors, and glass for the windows, help to create a suitable background for the exhibits. For the modern woodwork, window glass, and hardware, simple designs have been followed, and inconspicuous lighting arrangements have been installed.

The site of The Cloisters, on ledges of rock commanding a view of the Hudson River, brings to mind the situations of medieval church buildings at Mont-Saint-Michel, at Saint-Bertrand-de-Comminges, and at Basel. Rampart walls enclosing a courtyard provide a place from which to view the outside of the Fuentidueña apse and the magnificent surrounding landscape. The courtyard and the entrance driveways are paved with Belgian blocks, taken from New York streets, to suggest the cobblestones of old European towns.

The natural setting has been enhanced by extensive planting. Owing to the severity of the New York winter, landscaping with some of the trees native to the Mediterranean area was out of the question, but the flowering crab-apple trees on the southern slope of the Cloisters property recall the orchards and groves that often completely surrounded monasteries.

Within the walls of the building the landscaping is based on such medieval precedents as are available. In the Cuxa garden, iris and other plants known in the Middle Ages have been used in a semi-formal arrangement. Several apple trees are also planted there, as they were frequently grown in cloisters; some are still to be seen within the walls of the monastery of Saint-Michel-de-Cuxa. The walks were suggested by those of the central cloister in the plan of Saint-Gall. In the garden of the Trie Cloister, yews, English holly, myrtle, ivy, and various flowers have been planted somewhat as in old cloisters still extant abroad.

The garden in the Bonnefont Cloister has been conceived of as a medieval garden of herbs and flowers. The plan has no particular prototype but is based on medieval gardens as they are known to us in manuscript illuminations, tapestries, and paintings. Each variety of herb and flower has been labeled, so that visitors may identify them. Those growing in the Bonnefont Cloister are species mentioned in medieval texts and depicted in such works of art as the Unicorn tapestries. The list of herbs that Charlemagne gave directions to have grown in the imperial gardens has been particularly useful; it is preserved in *Capitulare de villis imperialibus*, issued in 812, and has often been published. Gradually the museum is collating various lists of medieval plants. A list of those growing in the Bonnefont Cloister garden, accompanied by a decorative plan, is available. A number of other books relating to the objects in the collection of The Cloisters, as well as pamphlets and copies of the *Bulletin* of the Metropolitan Museum, are also available.

SUGGESTED ITINERARY. The octagonal Entrance Hall, above which rises the tower, is the starting point for a visit to the Museum.

The arrangement of the exhibition areas and terraces is shown in the accompanying plans. They may be visited in the following order: *main floor*—the Romanesque Hall, the Fuentidueña Chapel, the Saint-Guilhem Cloister, the Langon Chapel, passageway to the West Terrace, the Chapter House from Pontaut, the Cuxa Cloister, the Nine Heroes Tapestry Room, the Early Gothic Hall, and stairway to the ground floor; *ground floor*—the Gothic Chapel, the Bonnefont

MAIN FLOOR

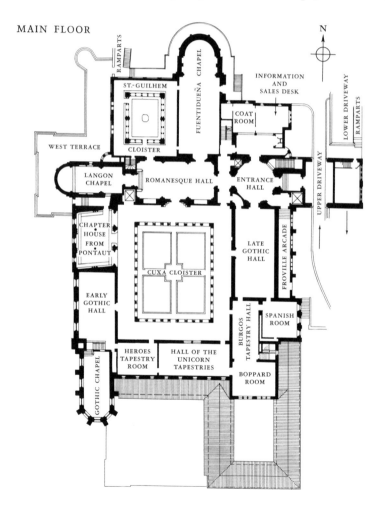

Cloister, the Trie Cloister, the Glass Gallery, the Treasury, and stairway to the main floor; *main floor*—the Boppard Room, the Hall of the Unicorn Tapestries, the Burgos Tapestry Hall (by way of the Cuxa Cloister), the Spanish Room, the Late Gothic Hall, the Froville Arcade.

It is suggested that, at least on the first visit, the exhibits be seen in consecutive order, beginning with the Romanesque and continuing with those of the early and late Gothic periods.

GROUND FLOOR

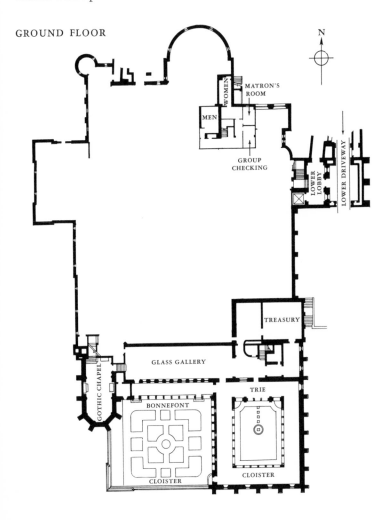

ELEMENTS OF THE ARCH

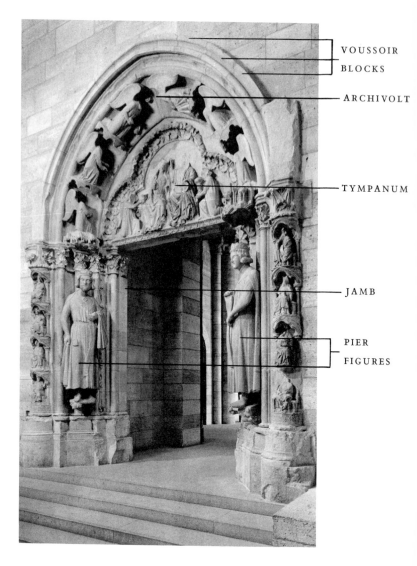

VOUSSOIR
BLOCKS

ARCHIVOLT

TYMPANUM

JAMB

PIER
FIGURES

ELEMENTS OF THE COLUMN

ABACUS
BLOCK

CAPITAL

SHAFT

BASE

PARAPET

THE ROMANESQUE HALL

Eusebius, writing in the fourth century, relates that the Emperor Constantine erected a great portal on one of his churches in Constantinople "in praise of the glory of Christ triumphant." Throughout the history of ecclesiastical architecture the entrance door to the cathedral or church has possessed a special importance. In medieval texts the church door is referred to as the gate of heaven, the portal of glory, and the triumphal gate. In early Christian times the lintels, tympana, and jambs of doors were seldom given figural sculpture, but a profound change occurred with the advent of the Romanesque style. Figures began to appear in pilasters on either side of porches; lintels and tympana were covered with reliefs. The development of the sculptured portal was not rapid. Hundreds of years were needed to produce the magnificent creations of the high Gothic period. The three portals incorporated into the Romanesque Hall exemplify this long evolution.

THE ENTRANCE DOORWAY has the round arch that is the most characteristic feature of the Romanesque style. Its proportions are monumental and solid. The decoration, although sparse, is so placed as to emphasize the important architectonic elements of the door. The keystone is emphasized by two carved animals—perhaps a boar and a fox. On the left side the capitals are skillfully carved with graceful birds feeding upon acanthus plants. The abacus blocks are sculptured with a hound pursuing a creature now almost entirely destroyed, and pairs of birds with grotesque heads. A series of confronted imaginary animals on the capitals of the right side are surmounted by a delicate acanthus motif.

15

1. Doorway from Moutiers-Saint-Jean. French, XIII century

We do not know the provenance of this doorway, but stylistic similarities to windows and portals in churches in Poitou suggest that region of France. The style appears to be of about the middle of the twelfth century.

THE REUGNY DOORWAY (fig. 2) leading into the Saint-Guilhem Cloister demonstrates, in its combination of Romanesque and Gothic elements, a transitional style. It comes from a small church in Reugny, in the upper Loire Valley, and dates from the end of the twelfth century.

The Gothic style appears in the pointed arch, which gives the portal a verticality and an upward movement that contrast with the round solidity of the Entrance Doorway. Whereas all decorative elements in the latter were subordinated to the architectural form, in the Reugny portal the columns, piers, and capitals have been given greater individual emphasis. Originally two statues, perhaps representing saints, formed the center columns. Only a fragment of one now remains; it was discovered buried near the door. This broken figure is still intrinsically a columnar support; later in the development from Romanesque to Gothic, figures began to be freestanding, no longer a part of the building itself, as may be seen in the doorway from Moutiers-Saint-Jean.

THE MOUTIERS-SAINT-JEAN DOORWAY (fig. 1). The magnificent thirteenth century Gothic doorway at the west end of the gallery, originally the entrance to the transept of the celebrated monastery of Moutiers-Saint-Jean in Burgundy, shows the high Gothic unison of architecture and sculpture. Each element bears an integral relationship to the whole. Moldings, ornament, and figure sculpture brilliantly carved and originally painted are worked into a single harmonious unit. The large capitals above the outer columns originally supported the vaulting of a porch that sheltered the doorway.

The most important figures are those of King Clovis on the left

2. Doorway from Reugny. French, late XII *century*

and his son King Clothar on the right, each standing in a canopied niche. According to tradition King Clovis, in the first year of his conversion to Christianity, probably 496, granted the monastery of Moutiers-Saint-Jean a charter of immunity that exempted it in perpetuity from royal and ecclesiastical jurisdiction; in addition he gave it as much land as could be encircled in a single day by a man riding an ass. His munificent donation was later confirmed by Clothar.

In the Coronation scene in the center of the tympanum the Virgin, treading on the tail of an adder, is crowned by Christ, who holds a disk carved as though studded with jewels. As prophesied in the Scriptures (Psalm 91:13), Christ treads upon the lion and the adder, symbols of evil. Angels bearing candlesticks kneel at either side. Above, on the voussoirs of the archivolt, are six adoring angels carrying various liturgical objects. The feathers on their wings are indicated with paint, perhaps as decoration or perhaps as guidelines for what the sculptor had yet to carve. The comparatively simple moldings of the main arch contrast with the elaborate trefoil cusped arch formed by grapevines that grow up the embrasures of the portal and frame the Coronation. The outer sides of the embrasures are flanked by columns in each of which there are figures seated in four canopied niches. These represent the biblical forerunners of Christ. The damaged condition of the figures makes identification in some cases difficult, but details that remain and comparison with similar groups make the following attributions likely. On the left, from bottom to top, are Elijah with the raven; David; Abraham with Isaac at his left and the angel with the ram at his right; and Saint John the Baptist with his long hair. On the right are Melchizedek beside an altar; Solomon holding the temple of Jerusalem; Moses with the horns and the brazen serpent; and Simeon holding the Christ child.

Moutiers-Saint-Jean is said to have been the oldest monastery in Burgundy; it appears to have been built before the time of Clovis. According to an eighteenth century account it was sacked twice in the sixteenth century: in 1567, when a group of Huguenots entered the monastery by a ruse and broke the statues of the founder princes, Clovis and Clothar, and again in 1584. It was severely damaged in the seventeenth century and was almost completely destroyed during the French Revolution.

In 1900 the statues of Clovis and Clothar were in a garden at Moutiers-Saint-Jean itself; later they were in the Manzi collection in Paris. Although the sculptures were missing from the portal for thirty years, there is no doubt that they are those made for the door-way. They accord with their present setting in style of carving, quality and color of stone, and measurements. Traces of old red paint on the mantle of Clovis, which show that these figures were once polychromed like most medieval statues, match similar traces on the doorway. The correspondence, in size and location, of a square iron pintle in the left-hand niche with parts of an iron fasten-ing in the back of the statue of Clovis prove conclusively the rela-tion of this figure to the niche.

A prosperous period of the abbey, under the protection of the dukes of Burgundy, began early in the thirteenth century with im-portant gifts of land and money. The monastery records reveal neither the gift of this doorway nor anything about its makers. However, the period of the most extensive building, from 1257 to about 1285, when the monastery fell badly into debt, coincides with the style of the doorway. This style, inspired by architectural sculpture on the cathedrals of Sens and Auxerre, is closely related to that of the doorway of the north transept of the church of Notre-Dame at Semur-en-Auxois, the main portal of the church of Notre-Dame at Cluny, the small tympanum from a former doorway of the north transept at the cathedral of Vézelay, and a tomb relief on the wall of the north side of the aisle of the church of Saint-Père-sous-Vézelay. All are the work of a single, homogeneous school of artists, who carried the great cathedral style to these outlying communities.

THE PORTAL LIONS, carved from a reddish Emilian mar-ble, flank the entrance to the Cuxa Cloister. They date from the early thirteenth century and are thought to have come from a church in the hamlet of Quattro Castella near Reggio Emilia in northern Italy. One of the lions digs its claws into a calf, the other holds a lamb.

Lions, either full size or half length like these, are incorporated into the portals of many Italian Romanesque churches, particu-

larly in Lombardy and Emilia. They may be placed on each side of
the door, freestanding or as supports for the columns of a porch;
sometimes they are used on the second story of a portico. The flat
surfaces on the backs of these two lions, each inset with a square hole
surrounded by traces of a circular area, indicate that originally the
lions supported columns.

Their date is problematical. They are similar in many respects to
a lion on the font in the baptistery in Parma that was carved by the
sculptor Antelami at the end of the twelfth century. They appear
to have been inspired by the Antelamesque type and probably date
from the first quarter of the thirteenth century.

*3, 4. Lion and winged dragon. Frescoes from San Pedro de
   Arlanza. Spanish, about 1220*

THE ARLANZA FRESCOES (figs. 3, 4). The two large
frescoes of the lion and the winged dragon were painted early in
the thirteenth century. They come from the walls of the chapter
house of the monastery of San Pedro de Arlanza, whose ruins are
not far from Burgos.

These two sections of the Arlanza frescoes are among the best
decorative Spanish wall paintings preserved. In the first a fierce,
Oriental-looking lion stands stiff-legged between a tree and an
arcade—the very image of enduring power; beneath him is a border of decorative fish. The lion has been placed facing the entrance
doorway to suggest his original location in the chapter house,
where two lion frescoes flanked the main portal. The border beneath the winged dragon is decorated with two confronting

harpies, a fox and a goat dancing to harp music played by an ass, two human figures, and two rabbits between them. In these vignettes one is tempted to read a story; it may be that the musical donkey reflects Aesop's fable of the ass who found a lyre but had not the skill to play it. Both panels are painted in true fresco: the paint applied swiftly and surely while the plaster is still fresh. Their style is extremely sophisticated; the freedom of the lines suggests the calligraphy of manuscript illumination, and in fact illuminated books often provided the models for large-scale fresco cycles. The lion is closely paralleled by several lions in the manuscript of the *Commentary on the Apocalypse* by Beatus of Liebana, in the Pierpont Morgan Library in New York, which was illuminated in the royal Cistercian convent of Las Huelgas on the outskirts of Burgos. The similarity of the manuscript lions to that of the fresco suggests strongly that the date 1220, written in the colophon of the manuscript, is a reasonable one for the frescoes.

The history of the monastery of San Pedro is well documented. Tradition ascribes its founding both to Wallia, a Visigothic king, and with more probability to the great count of Castile, Fernán González, who bestowed favors on the monastery early in the tenth century. The church was begun in the eleventh century; building continued in the twelfth and thirteenth, and parts were changed in the fifteenth and sixteenth centuries. In the chapter house a room originally about 34 feet square and 12 feet high was decorated from floor to ceiling with frescoes representing large and fantastic animals, framed with ornamental borders. In the eighteenth century the room was completely remodeled to permit the erection of a monumental staircase. Those frescoes that were not demolished were roughened with picks so that the new layer of plaster would stick to the old surface. This explains the pocked appearance of the paintings today. When Church and conventual property in Spain was sequestered in 1835–1837, the monastery at Arlanza became national property. In 1845 practically all the buildings were sold by national decree to a private citizen. When the roof of the chapter house collapsed and the plaster that for years had protected the walls began to crumble, little by little the paintings were exposed to the elements. The Arlanza frescoes were removed to safety prior to 1929; otherwise at present very little would remain of this important series.

The process of removing frescoes from old walls begins with cleaning the surface of the fresco; then canvas or some other cloth is applied to the surface with a paste that binds the fresco more securely to it than to the wall. The canvas and fresco are then cut, and the fresco loosened from the wall with a knife or spatula and rolled. A layer of canvas is attached to the back of the fresco, and the protecting canvas on the front is removed with a solvent that affects neither the fresco nor the paste of the lining canvas. The canvas with the fresco on the front is then ready for mounting.

THE ADORATION GROUP (fig. 6). The four large figures in the niche above the door leading to the Cuxa Cloister represent the Adoration of the Magi. They come from the church of Nuestra Señora de la Llama in the town of Cerezo de Riotirón a few miles south of Burgos. They are thus from the same locality as the Arlanza frescoes and are almost contemporary with them. These sculptures show perhaps better than any others in The Cloisters the monumentality and the vigor of the late Romanesque period.

The figure of the Virgin and Child dominates the composition. Joseph (fig. 5) sits dozing at the Virgin's left side and two kings kneel at her right. Three kings usually take part in the Adoration, but a photograph of the Cerezo group in its original setting, in a niche above an arch west of the south portal of the church, shows the composition exactly as it appears here. Thus there is no reason to suppose that one of the kings has been lost. The marked characteristic of the style is the combination of the monumental heaviness of the forms with the intricacy of the draperies that flow

5. *Joseph.*
Detail of
Figure 6

restlessly over the blocklike figures. These linear folds reveal the anatomy of the figures and at the same time create a series of decorative patterns.

The four figures are similar to sculptures in the area around Burgos, notably the tympana of the churches at Moradillo de Sedano and Gredilla de Sedano, and the Adoration group at Butrera. The inscription on a capital on the façade of the church at Moradillo, IN ERA MCCXXVI (1226: i. e. 1188 by the Gregorian or modern calendar), provides evidence for the approximate dating of the Cerezo Adoration.

6. *The Adoration of the Magi. Sculpture from Cerezo de Riotirón. Spanish,*
 about 1188

THE TORSO OF CHRIST, a fragment of a Crucifixion, is one of the finest Romanesque sculptures in The Cloisters. The head that once belonged to it is one of the treasures of the Louvre. The painted wood figure comes from the town of Lavaudieu, near

Brioude in the province of Auvergne in central France; it dates from the third or fourth decade of the twelfth century. The simplified yet graceful curves of the anatomy and the delicate, flattened folds of the loincloth, which fall into a series of soft zigzags, are characteristic of the best Auvergne style. The torso, once obscured by accumulations of dirt and post-medieval polychromy, has been cleaned, revealing two layers of medieval painting. In the twelfth century the loincloth was blue, with appliqué ornaments of clustered squares probably made of precious metal. Only slight traces of the blue remain, but the square patterns where the applied ornaments were once attached can be clearly seen. In Gothic times the blue was painted over with scarlet and green which, in turn, were decorated with checks outlined in black and yellow; this layer of paint is still clearly visible. The flesh tones of the torso are now as they were when the figure was originally made. The story of painting and repainting through the centuries as shown here is typical of many of the sculptures at The Cloisters.

THE VIRGIN AND SAINT JOHN (figs. 7, 8), two wood figures flanking the Auvergne Christ, do not belong to the original composition. They are Italian and compare in general to a series of wood Crucifixion groups made in workshops in Lombardy and Tuscany in the first half of the thirteenth century. The flatness of the figures and the hardness of the draperies indicate the influence of metalwork or perhaps Italo–Byzantine ivory carvings.

The statues are carved in soft red pine. When they were made the wood was covered with a layer of gesso composed of fine gypsum and glue. For the modeling of the heads and some of the drapery folds, canvas was placed over a coarse plastic material. For the garments, the ground was overlaid with a very thin layer of tin foil that reflected light through the colored oil glazes with which it was covered.

7, 8. The Virgin and Saint John. Italian, XIII *century*

THE FUENTIDUEÑA CHAPEL

The Spanish Romanesque apse (fig. 9) comes from the church of San Martín in Fuentidueña, a village about a hundred miles north of Madrid, in the province of Segovia. Built of well-cut blocks of golden limestone, with carved capitals, corbels, pier figures, and moldings, the apse is in complete contrast with the rest of San Martín, which was constructed mainly of rubble and plaster and was already a ruin in 1865. The ruined portions of the church, consisting of the broken-down walls of the nave and parts of the tower, still stand on the hillside above the village of Fuentidueña. In the reconstruction at The Cloisters, a modern nave of almost the same size replaces the original. Its beamed wood ceiling is of a type known to have been used in many Segovian churches of the Romanesque period. The apse is on loan from Spain.

The plan of San Martín—one nave and apse with no transepts and no side aisles—is common in small Romanesque churches in Segovia. The sturdy construction of the apse, combined with the grace of the rising triumphal arch and the majesty of the half dome, is typical of the best in Romanesque architecture anywhere. The three windows, also typically Romanesque, are mere slits on the outside, becoming wide on the inside, with splayed jambs. The openings are very narrow, for no glass was used, and the interior had to be protected as much as possible from the weather. The two small niches in the wall probably served some liturgical purpose; the one on the left may have held the two cruets of water and of wine used in the Mass, the one on the right the basin and ewer used in the priest's ceremonial washing of hands.

The apse is richly decorated with sculpture carved in limestone of finer grain and grayer color than the blocks used in the main

structure. The large pier figures, Saint Martin (fig. 13) on the left
and the Annunciation on the right, form the strongest accents of
the interior. Sculptures of such importance in size and workmanship are common on façades of churches, but only very rarely do
they appear incorporated into an apse as they are here. Since
they serve no functional purpose in the architecture, it may be that
they were first intended to be column figures flanking a doorway,
but because of some change in plan were placed in the apse instead,
upon simple uncarved blocks to achieve the correct height.

Saint Martin, bishop of Tours, was among the most venerated
saints of the Middle Ages, and the church of San Martín at Fuentidueña was one of thousands dedicated to him. He is shown here as
a bishop, wearing a miter and highly stylized priestly garments that
fall in angular folds at the hems. He stands on two animals difficult
to identify but probably representing the evil forces over which he

9. Apse from San Martín at Fuentidueña. Spanish, about 1160

triumphed. His head, lost for many years, was found in the home of one of the townspeople of Fuentidueña and has now been restored to its original position.

The figure of Saint Martin is formal and static. The Annunciation group opposite, on the other hand, is vital and full of movement, showing the sculptor's ability to fit the narrative into a restricted and difficult space. Although much is missing from the two figures, enough remains to convey a sense of the urgency of the angel's message. Gabriel leans toward the Virgin with bent knee and drapery folds accentuating his forward motion; Mary, with raised arms and uplifted head, appears to listen actively to his words. The clinging garments reveal the slender limbs of the figures; the feet follow in position the square shape of the base of the column. The capital above the Annunciation represents the Nativity in the traditional Romanesque interpretation. Mary lies in bed and the Christ child in the manger above her; the ox and the ass bend their heads over the Child, and two hooded shepherds holding staves approach from the left. Below the Annunciation is a typical medieval hell mouth: devils thrust the naked souls of the damned into the jaws of a monstrous head.

The two large capitals supporting the triumphal arch also have biblical subjects: on the left is the Adoration of the Magi, on the right Daniel in the Lions' Den (fig. 10). The rest of the capitals represent real or fantastic creatures (see fig. 11) probably derived from bestiaries. Among those identified are centaurs on the capitals of the blind arcades, basilisks pecking at a bald head in the window on the left, and sirens wearing caps in the window at the right. All the capitals have a certain primitive vigor; their strong dark-and-light patterns form varied accents at functional points in the architecture. The crisp moldings carved in billet, interlace, and floral patterns also emphasize the architectural structure of the apse and contribute in large measure to its beauty.

The exterior of the apse is also ornamented with carved mold-

10, 11. Capitals from the interior of the Fuentidueña apse

ings, elaborate capitals, two pier sculptures, and a series of amusing corbels. Among the latter are several figures playing musical instruments, a castle, an ape, Adam with his fig leaf, and the tree of knowledge of good and evil complete with forbidden fruit and the serpent. The window capitals, like those inside, are carved with real and imaginary birds and beasts. Among those that can be recognized are mermaids holding their double fishtails, two pairs of dogs entangled in vines that issue from a monstrous head, and two pairs of birds eating grapes. Of the large capitals supporting the cornice, one has a deeply undercut basketwork pattern; another is decorated with four standing sirens, and a third, the most beautiful of all, with two pairs of lions bending over, heads together and bodies forming graceful sweeping curves. (The latter is a cast of the original, which has been placed inside the building for its better protection and so that it may be studied closely.)

The grotesque fat man serving as a column for the blind arches on the east side of the apse is the most puzzling of all the sculptures.

He may be an Atlas figure, a survival from classical times; perhaps his very heavy body seemed to the sculptor a suitable form to carry the weight of the masonry above. The group of acrobatic figures (fig. 14) supporting the blind arches on the opposite side of the apse is much better preserved and more successful as architectural sculpture. Above the upturned head of a lion a crouching man supports two kneeling figures with a column on their shoulders. This dynamic group is surmounted by a capital with confronting turtledoves. (The original group has been placed inside the chapel; a cast replaces it on the outside.)

The capitals and corbels are the work of at least two different artists. The Daniel capital on the interior is characteristic of one; Daniel's face is flat, with round bulging eyes and straight mouth with thick spread lips. The style of the second artist is apparent in the Magi capital, where the faces are more extensively modeled, the eyes are carved with deep round holes to suggest dark pupils, and the mouths have thin lips, the upper one v-shaped. Probably a third and possibly a fourth artist produced the large column figures on both exterior and interior, for these show greater technical skill and sophistication in design. All the sculptures were probably carved by a single workshop; it would be quite natural for the master to have directed all the work and to have executed the most important pieces himself.

The San Martín sculptures have a certain regional character with indications of influence from outside the province and even outside Spain. The Annunciation group is very close in style to a statue in nearby Sepúlveda probably representing Saint John the Evangelist, but the column of acrobatic figures from the west blind arches is more nearly related to north Italian sculptures. The motif of lions with heads together and bodies bent over can be traced to San Isidoro of León, whence it spread to San Vicente and San Pedro of Avila. On the other hand, deep drill holes for the pupils of eyes occur in sculptures from as far away as Burgundy in France or Bari in

12. Interior of the Fuentidueña apse

southern Italy. Fuentidueña was not far from the great pilgrimage route to Santiago de Compostela, and the sculptors of San Martín must have been in contact with the artistic currents that were interchanged all along the Way of Saint James.

It is difficult to date the apse. There are no records of the building of San Martín nor of the parish church of San Miguel at Fuentidueña, which is similar in style and probably of the same date. There are relatively few records of Fuentidueña itself. There is evidence that in the twelfth century it was a fortified town of strategic importance to the Christian kings of Castile in their struggles against the Moors. The bishopric of Segovia, to which Fuentidueña belonged, was reconstituted in 1123 after a lapse of three centuries. The village is mentioned in documents signed by Alfonso VII (reigned 1135–1157) and Alfonso VIII (reigned 1158–1214), but after 1206 its name disappears except for casual references in documents of the fifteenth century. It was Alfonso VII who gave the main impulse for the construction of religious houses in the region. Very likely those built in areas that were strategically important for a short period, as was Fuentidueña, were begun before or at least shortly after his death in 1157. Most of the related monuments mentioned here were built in the first half of the twelfth century, but a date of about 1160 seems reasonable for the San Martín apse; it is probably contemporary with the church of Santa Maria de la Sierra in Sepúlveda and earlier than most of the churches in the city of Segovia.

It is not known for what kind of religious community the church of San Martín was built. Since there are ruins of an apparently important castle adjacent to the site of the church, there is reason to believe that San Martín may have been the castle chapel.

THE TREDÓS FRESCO. The Romanesque fresco of the Virgin and Child with the three Magi and the archangels Michael and Gabriel (see fig. 12) was originally in the apse of the small Cata-

13, 14. Saint Martin and acrobatic figures.
 Pier sculptures of the Fuentidueña apse

lan church of San Juan de Tredós in the Pyrenees. The enthroned Virgin, unusually well preserved, had been protected by a baroque altarpiece that was destroyed during the Spanish Civil War in the 1930s.

In many ways the fresco recalls Byzantine mosaics: in the rich play of color and the sophisticated stylization of the figures, in the costumes and jeweled throne, and above all in the interpretation of the Virgin as the Mother of God, austere, remote, transcendental. In draftsmanship and technique it is similar to the eleventh century Italo-Byzantine wall paintings of San Vincenzo in Galliano, near Como in Lombardy. The motif of the two archangels presenting petitions of the faithful before the heavenly throne may also derive from Galliano. Saint Michael's scroll is obliterated, but Gabriel's still bears the inscription *Postulacius*: one who pleads.

The painter of the fresco is known as the Pedret Master because of the cycle of frescoes he painted for the church of San Quirce of Pedret in Catalonia, some of which are in the museum at Solsona and others in the Museum of Catalan Art in Barcelona. Authorities differ by centuries in dating the work of this master. Some place it as early as the tenth, others as late as the thirteenth century. One iconographic detail of the Tredós fresco suggests an earlier rather than a later date: the three Magi, labeled MEL[C]HIOR, BALDASAR, and GASPA[R], wear caps instead of crowns. It is probable that the fresco dates from about 1130–1150.

Like the Arlanza lion and dragon in the Romanesque Hall, this is a true fresco, painted on fresh plaster while the surface was still wet, with details such as the ultramarine blue added in tempera later. The technique demanded absolute sureness of hand, for once the artist had brushed his colors on the wet plaster he could not make corrections or alterations. The Pedret Master was one of the greatest of the Romanesque fresco painters of any land, and this Virgin and Child is one of his finest achievements.

*15. The Healing of the Blind Man and the Raising of Lazarus.
Fresco from San Baudelio de Berlanga. Spanish,* XII *century*

THE SAN BAUDELIO DE BERLANGA FRESCOES.

The two frescoes with scenes from the life of Christ are part of a
series of wall paintings from the hermitage church of San Baudelio,
situated in a barren countryside near the small Castilian town of
Casillas de Berlanga, about eighty-five miles northeast of Madrid.
One represents the Temptation of Christ, and the other, two of the
miracles, the Healing of the Blind Man and the Raising of Lazarus
(fig. 15). Both have dramatic force and both show originality in
the telling of the story. In the Raising of Lazarus, Mary and
Martha, instead of standing quietly by their brother's grave or
kneeling before Christ as they usually do, participate in the miracle
by lifting the heavy lid of the sarcophagus. In the Temptation
scene, the third temptation of Christ is replaced by an angel telling
the devil to be gone. Since the figure of Christ is drawn and interpreted differently in the two frescoes, it would seem that they are
the work of two different artists.

Unlike the Tredós fresco, these murals are largely in *fresco secco*:
only the basic outlines of the design and the background of traditional bands of color were painted in true fresco on fresh, wet

plaster. In the *secco* technique the colors, mixed with limewater as a binder, were applied to a moistened plaster wall. Fine details and areas requiring stronger colors than were possible with limewater were often added later in pigments tempered with egg, casein, or size. The pigments here, except for the black and white, are all earth colors.

The hermitage church, in the Mozarabic style, was built in the tenth or eleventh century. The frescoes, however, were added later, probably in the second half of the twelfth century.

The San Baudelio frescoes, one of the most complete cycles of Romanesque wall paintings in existence, were brought to this country in 1920. The Last Supper and the Three Marys at the Sepulcher are in the Boston Museum of Fine Arts; the Marriage at Cana and the Entry into Jerusalem are in the Indianapolis museum. A group of six secular scenes, including an elephant, a bear, and a man with a bow and arrow shooting a stag, was bought by the Metropolitan Museum and sent to the Prado in Madrid as an exchange loan for the Fuentidueña apse. Others are privately owned.

THE ALTAR. Besides the actual building with its decorations, various pieces of church furniture were essential to the established performance of the sacraments. Of these the altar was always the most important. In the larger churches there were often several. Some were made of gold and enriched with precious stones, some were painted or sculptured, others were ornamented with enamel plaques. Often in Spain, particularly in the region of Lérida, raised and painted gesso work, simulating more costly materials, was applied to a wood foundation much as frosting is forced from a pastry bag.

The altar frontal in this chapel is one of the best surviving examples in that technique, although the colors have by this time lost much of their brilliance. The Virgin and Child are shown in the center of the panel, enthroned in a mandorla supported by four angels; eight apostles standing in arched niches complete the composition, which is framed by an inscription and borders with lions passant alternating with double palmettes. The inscription gives in Latin the names of six saints: Simon and Jude, Matthew and John, Thomas and Barnabas. The frontal comes from the parish church of Ginestarre de Cardós in Catalonia. Another, in the same style and technique, from the same church and dated 122[3?], is in the Barcelona museum.

THE CRUCIFIX (fig. 16), a twelfth century Spanish sculpture, is comparable to the finest medieval figures of Christ in Europe, such as the famous Courajod Christ in the Louvre. It is said to have been found in a convent of Santa Clara in the Spanish province of León, near Palencia. The figure of Christ is practically intact. Three of the arms of the cross were at some time shortened; these have now been restored in order to obtain the original relation in scale between the figure and the cross; even the iron fastenings holding the body to the cross are original.

In Romanesque crucifixes the almost horizontal arms, the stylized, symmetrical anatomy, and the flattened folds of the drapery gave to the figures of Christ a rare spiritual composure. Later treatments of the subject became more emotional and sometimes painfully realistic. The dignity and the spirituality of this Spanish crucifix are heightened by the contrast between the crown, symbol of Christ's regality, and the loincloth.

The color scheme, like the carving, is simple and direct. The hair and beard are black, the diadem is gold studded with painted red and green jewels; the loincloth, once blue, is bordered in gold. The cross itself, which retains most of its original paint, is dark green with a gilded border studded with cabochonlike ornaments, blue, red, and green in repeated series. Probably the ends of the crossbar were painted with figures of Mary and John, and

16. Crucifix. Spanish, XII century

the hand of God, the moon and the sun, or some other symbol may
have been shown at the top. The letters INRI were probably painted
directly on the cross or on a separate panel placed above the head of
Christ. On the back of the cross the Lamb of God is painted in the
center, and at the ends of the crossbar are portions of two of the
four symbols of the Evangelists.

The figure of Christ is made of walnut and the cross of red pine. In places parchment was used over the wood to cover joints and to give a better surface on which to apply gesso. The entire surface of the crucifix is covered with gesso; in certain areas this is thick and has actually been modeled.

In the convent of Santa Clara, according to tradition, the crucifix hung behind an eighteenth century altar in a niche at the east end of a chapel. An inscription in stone placed above the crucifix supposedly recorded its donation to the church in the year 1047; as this date is not consistent with the style of the piece, it is possible that it was incorrectly deciphered and actually read 1147. The latter would be more consistent with certain Spanish monuments of known provenance with which the crucifix may be compared, including several in the Morgan collection of the Metropolitan Museum. One of these is a silver and silver-gilt processional cross of the twelfth century from the church of San Salvador de Fuentes in the province of Oviedo. The figure of Christ on the Cloisters crucifix is practically identical to an ivory figure of Christ on the interior of a famous reliquary made for Bishop Gonzalo Menendez (1162–1175), in the Cámara Santa of the cathedral of Oviedo.

THE LION FROM ZAMORA, a relief in which Christ is symbolized as the Lion of the Tribe of Judah, was one of a pair set high up on the gable of the portal of the now demolished church of San Leonardo at Zamora in Spain. This relief and its companion piece, a lioness, were used, according to custom, as the guardians of the church doorway. The lion tramples on a serpent, symbol of Satan; in the background are Christ crowning the Virgin, attended by the archangel Gabriel, and Saint Leonard of Aquitaine freeing two prisoners.

The considerable remains of color are unusual for exterior stone sculpture. They show strikingly to what degree most medieval sculpture is now destitute of color and how important this final embellishment was in producing the desired effect. From several inscriptions on the original portal the relief may be dated about the middle of the thirteenth century.

THE BAPTISMAL FONT of black calcite with its four heads projecting beyond the series of arcades dates around 1200; it was made in the area near Tongres and Maastricht where the river Meuse crosses the border between Belgium and Holland.

The arcade with animals supporting the columns and the series of recessed arcades with animal corbels are similar to architectural elements of the late twelfth century in the Servatius church at Maastricht and to those of the early thirteenth century cloister at Tongres. The bold, strong heads with their flamboyant mustaches are similar to sculptures in Maastricht carved around the turn of the thirteenth century.

THE SAINT-GUILHEM CLOISTER

T HE Saint-Guilhem Cloister (fig. 17) has been planned around the unusual and magnificent series of capitals, shafts, and columns from the cloister of the once famous Benedictine abbey of Saint-Guilhem-le-Désert, not far from Montpellier. The present architectural setting was suggested by the cloister of Saint-Trophîme at Arles and those at Montmajour and Saint-Rémy. The high wall, like that at Arles, above the arcades around the court makes possible the use of a skylight which is not conspicuous from the walks. By this means the delicate material is protected from the elements and yet can be seen in natural light coming from overhead as it does in uncovered cloister courts.

The Saint-Guilhem sculptures are the product of several highly skilled craftsmen, each working out his designs in his own technique and style. The majority are transitional between the conventionalized, formalized Romanesque tradition and the new freer and more naturalistic Gothic manner. In the dexterity of the cutting, in the freedom and perfection of the ornamentation, and above all in the play of light and dark between the intricate surface patterns and the deeply undercut background areas, this is supreme chisel work.

These sculptures show the variety within unity that the Middle Ages loved so well. Several of the capitals (see fig. 18) are derived from the classic Corinthian type with curling acanthus leaves, perhaps suggested by surviving Roman monuments in the south of France. On one the acanthus leaves sweep spirally around the bowl-like form. Another is closely patterned with flat heart-shaped leaves of the black bryony vine. Still another is covered with

43

a lacework of vines, leaves, and tendrils. Among the historiated capitals are one representing the Presentation in the Temple, designed and sculptured in the Romanesque manner, and another, representing sinners being led in chains to the mouth of hell (fig. 19), which is early Gothic in style.

The abaci also are ornamented in a variety of imaginative designs. On one (fig. 18) the tendrils of a vine end in human heads. A ribbon meanders in angular folds on another, suggesting a Greek fret pattern translated into the French medieval idiom. Several of the column shafts are carefully sculptured. One is decorated with broad acanthus leaves in low, flat relief; another is a conventionalized rendering of the trunk of a palm tree; a third is covered with an intricate chevron pattern. The pilaster decorated with acanthus spirals and strange fruits is perhaps the most memorable of the elements: even a goldsmith's work is not more precise.

The abbey of Saint-Guilhem-le-Désert was founded in 804 by Guilhem, count of Toulouse, and until the twelfth century was called Gellone after the once lonely valley in which it stood. Guilhem was one of Charlemagne's paladins and hero of many chansons de geste. The jongleurs told how he captured Nîmes by bringing his soldiers within the walls hidden in empty wine barrels; how he freed Rome from a besieging pagan army but lost the tip of his nose in the battle; how he was imprisoned by a Saracen king and escaped with the aid of the Saracen's wife, whom he later married. Although much of his reputation is legendary, it is historical fact that in 806 Guilhem became a monk in the same monastery he had founded. When he died a few years later, so the records say, the bells of all the churches in the province rang without any hand touching their ropes. Guilhem became a saint as well as a hero. The combination had powerful appeal, and pilgrims flocked to his shrine. By the early twelfth century Saint-Guilhem-le-Désert was a regular stop on the great pilgrimage route through Toulouse to Compostela, and in 1165 it was included among seven minor

17. Arcades and garden court of the Saint-Guilhem Cloister

pilgrimages imposed as penance upon the Albigensian heretics. One of its treasures was the famous relic of the True Cross given by the Patriarch of Jerusalem to Charlemagne in 800 and presented by him to Guilhem.

The pilgrims brought gifts of all kinds, and the abbey flourished. Sometime before 1206, according to a cartulary of the monastery, a "new cloisters" was built. Two plans dated 1656, before the cloister was dismantled, indicate that the "new cloisters" consisted of an entire upper gallery and two sides of the earlier cloister on the ground-floor level. It is almost certain that the stonework from Saint-Guilhem now at The Cloisters came from either the upper or lower arcades of this "new cloisters" completed before 1206.

In the religious wars the monastery suffered at the hands of the Calvinists, who took possession of the place in 1568. During the French Revolution the property was sold; first it was used for a cotton mill and then for a tannery. These undertakings were not successful, and finally the cloister was sold to a stonemason who exploited it as a quarry for many years. Some of the sculptured parts were gathered together in the church of Saint-Guilhem in the third quarter of the nineteenth century by the Abbé Léon Vinas, who wrote what is still the best monograph on the subject. Most of the fragments, however, had been brought together by Pierre Yon Vernière, onetime justice of the peace at Aniane. He placed them in his garden as decoration and used many of the finest columns to support grape arbors. By 1906 these carvings had been brought to Paris, and later they were bought and sent to the United States by George Grey Barnard. He, perhaps better than anyone of his day, recognized in them the best sculptural traditions.

THE CORBELS AND WINDOWS. The ten humorous, grotesque corbels from the abbey of Notre-Dame-de-la-Grande-Sauve (la Sauve-Majeure) near Bordeaux are used in the Saint-Guilhem Cloister to support the ribs and cornice of the vaults over the cloister walks exactly as are similar ones at Montmajour. Orig-

18. Capital from Saint-Guilhem-le-Désert. French, before 1206

inally these corbels, which are of the same period as the Saint-Guilhem carvings, were supporting members for an exterior cornice. The columns in the two windows overlooking the Hudson River probably also come from la Sauve, where they may have been used in the former cloister.

THE AUTUN ANGEL was once a voussoir block from the north portal of the Romanesque cathedral of Saint-Lazare at Autun in Burgundy. The church was begun about 1120 as a shrine for the relics of Lazarus; it was completed except for minor details by 1146, when the relics were transferred with elaborate ceremonies to the new edifice. In 1776 the canons of the cathedral pronounced the twelfth century sculpture of the doorways to be "of Gothic [meaning barbaric] bastardy" and "in poor taste." So the great west portal of the Last Judgment was covered over with bricks and plaster and the north portal of the Raising of Lazarus was almost entirely dismantled to make way for a wooden doorway carved in eighteenth century designs more pleasing to the canons. Fortunately several of the sculptured stones were used as building blocks in houses in the town and have been recovered. The Cloisters angel is one of the most nearly complete. The elongated proportions of the figure, the thin drapery fluttering at the hem with the folds indicated by fine calligraphic lines, the pearled borders, the feathered wings, and the deep undercutting relate this angel to those of the Last Judgment on the west portal of the cathedral. This portal, signed by a certain Gislebertus, is one of the finest monuments of Romanesque sculpture in France.

THE RELIEF FROM REIMS. Three small clerics standing in attitudes of arrested movement, framed by columns, were probably part of a funeral procession carved on a tomb. The patterns of the drapery folds, the modeling of the heads, and the design of the little turrets above the columns are related to the twelfth century sculptures set into the north portal of Reims cathedral. It is thought that the cathedral sculptures were originally parts of an imposing tomb monument; since the Cloisters relief was sold in Reims, there is a possibility that it once formed part of the decoration for the same tomb. Even if this cannot be proven, the style of the carving indicates a north French provenance of the second half of the twelfth century.

THE LUCCA FIGURES. In contrast to the French Romanesque sculptures in this cloister are two marble figures of the late twelfth or early thirteenth century that, according to local history, come from the church of San Agostino in the pilgrimage center of Lucca. The seated bearded figure holding a scroll between his knees is the typical representation of an Old Testament prophet. The fragmentary standing figure with a large water flask under his right arm is less easily identified. He may represent Joseph on the Flight into Egypt, or the risen Christ on the way to Emmaus.

19. Capital from Saint-Guilhem-le-Désert. French, before 1206

We do not know the original placement of the two figures. They could have been installed on the façade of a church, in the tympana of doorways, or in arcades. But their size and the unweathered condition of the marble suggest that they were once incorporated into a large pulpit or tribune.

Although the two sculptures are not by the same artist, they were probably produced in the same workshop. Both have a distinctive ropelike treatment of certain draperies, particularly the standing figure, and show extensive use of the drill. Fragments in the same style, representing angels and the three kings, are in museums in Florence and Lucca. The sculptures have affinities with the products of the workshop of Biduinus, a master active around Pisa and Lucca in the second half of the twelfth century.

THE FLORENTINE RELIEF of the Annunciation, in fine Maremma marble, is one of seven panels that adorned a famous Romanesque pulpit once in the Florentine church of San Piero Scheraggio. The other six reliefs are today in a pulpit in the small church of San Leonardo in Arcetri on the south bank of the Arno.

The Annunciation is an excellent example of Florentine sculpture of about 1200. The use of inlaid dark green serpentine or *verde
di Prato* for the decorative elements and even the eyes of the figures
is typical. The combination of inlay work and relief sculpture, on
the other hand, is unique in Tuscan Romanesque sculpture.

A number of fascinating legends have grown up around the San
Piero pulpit. One story is that it was made "in a very remote age"
in Fiesole—perhaps not by mortals but by angels. It is also said to
have been captured from Fiesole by the Florentines in 1010. Other
traditions relate that Dante preached from it in the thirteenth
century and Saint Antoninus and Savonarola in the fifteenth.

Dedicated in 1068, San Piero was the seat of Florentine government until 1298, when the Palazzo Vecchio was constructed. In
1410 its left side aisle was removed and walled up; around 1580 the
part of the Uffizi nearest the Palazzo Vecchio was built around its
ancient walls. Today the entrance hall of the Uffizi Gallery is the
center of the old San Piero nave, and parts of the medieval arcade
are still visible there. The church was deconsecrated in 1782 and
the pulpit was removed and rebuilt in San Leonardo in Arcetri.
Since the Annunciation relief is not mentioned in the first publica-
tion of the pulpit nor shown in the earliest engraving of it in 1755,
it was presumably separated from the other six reliefs at an early
date, possibly in 1410.

THE FOUNTAIN in the center of the cloister was once a capital in the church of Saint-Sauveur at Figeac. The capital was later
made into a font, as was a companion piece still at Figeac. In style it
is earlier than the Saint-Guilhem carvings; it may even have been
carved as early as the late eleventh century. As it was used to support heavy architectural members that were high above the floor,
its deeply cut ornamentation is more rugged than that of the delicate cloister capitals.

THE LANGON CHAPEL

THE old stonework incorporated in the walls of this Romanesque chapel (fig. 20) comes from the twelfth century church of Notre-Dame-du-Bourg at Langon, near Bordeaux. The present right wall (formerly the south wall of the choir) with its two columns and single window has been installed with little variation from the original Romanesque arrangement. The present left wall has been reconstructed with stonework that harmonizes with the original parts of the right side and into which are incorporated two large capitals, one column, and a smaller capital from the old chapel (see explanatory label in the chapel). The cornice at Langon was 23 feet 6½ inches above the floor of the choir; in the present installation it is 17 feet. The width of the interior has been decreased proportionately from 23 feet 3 inches at Langon to 17 feet 3 ⅜ inches here. Thus the original elements are readily visible from the floor and predominate over the modern work.

The capitals from Langon do not appear to have a religious significance or any particular story to tell. The bending half-length figures recall Greek atlantes and caryatids in their ceaseless effort to support the weight above them. Although the crowned heads (fig. 23) that look away from the altar cannot be verified as actual portraits, they may possibly represent Henry II of England and his wife Eleanor of Aquitaine, royal patrons who visited in 1155 the monastery of Notre-Dame-de-la-Grande-Sauve of which the church at Langon was a dependency. The various heads are beautifully carved, with unusual emphasis on simple planes. In contrast to other sculptures of their period they are strikingly lifelike. The decorative elements of the abacus blocks and the cornice moldings are conventionalized leaf and snail motifs well suited to the vigorous, stylized carving of the heads and figures.

No traces of original painted decoration have been found on the brownish white limestone of the church walls. The first of several coats of whitewash may have been applied soon after the building was completed.

Gaufredus, abbot of Notre-Dame-de-la-Grande-Sauve, ordered the church at Langon to be founded in 1126, the year in which he became bishop of Bazas. The church must have been well under way before 1155, as it had received important gifts prior to then. Raymond of Dax (Raimundus Aquensis), librarian of la Sauve, was in charge of its construction. The town of Langon, which resisted such famous soldiers as Du Guesclin in 1374 and Montgoméry in 1566, was involved for many centuries in wars and rebellions; Notre-Dame suffered accordingly. At the time this stonework was acquired for The Cloisters all that remained of the church was a portion of the choir, which had been divided into two stories by a wood floor. The lower part was used as a stable, and the upper rooms, which had been a Jacobin club during the French Revolution, were later a dance hall and a moving-picture theater.

The twelfth century architecture of Notre-Dame-du-Bourg is not unlike that of other buildings in the region. Such motifs as the snails are to be found in larger buildings, especially the cathedral of Bordeaux. But the sculptural decorations at Langon are not stylistically related to those of the other churches listed in a papal bull of 1246 as dependent on la Grande-Sauve.

THE CIBORIUM. In the early Christian church the ciborium was a canopy over the altar, supported on columns. It is also known as a baldachin, or baldacchino, from Baldacco, the Italian name for

20. The Langon Chapel

Baghdad, which exported to the West elaborate textiles used for altar canopies. From this tabernacle-like structure hung the receptacle that held the consecrated wafer. In time the word ciborium came to denote the container for the wafer itself.

The marble ciborium with gold and colored mosaic inlay decoration, now exhibited here, was until at least 1889 in the former church of Santo Stefano near Fiano Romano near Rome. The roofs, which are set in their original beveled grooves, are restorations that have the same dimensions and angles as those shown in a photograph of the ciborium when it was still standing at Santo Stefano in an apse similar in proportion to the Langon Chapel. Most existing ciboria of this type are still in Rome and the surrounding provinces. An almost identical one in the church of Sant' Andrea in Flumine near Ponzano was made about 1150 by the Roman marble workers Nicolaus Ranucius and his sons Giovanni and Guitonne.

THE ROMANESQUE VIRGIN enthroned (fig. 21) is one of the few surviving wood sculptures in the round from that vital Burgundian school which in the twelfth century produced such magnificent portals as those of Vézelay and Autun and infused new life into the art of all France. This statue is closely related in style to the sculptures in the doorway of the cathedral of Saint-Lazare at Autun, which were executed about 1120–1132 and signed by one Gislebertus. Here are the same attenuation of form, the same linear quality, the same treatment of thin drapery with folds indicated by parallel ridges set close together, the same upward swirl of the garments at the hem as if blown by a sudden gust of wind. The Virgin's head, like those on the Autun portal, has heavy-lidded eyes, straight mouth, and softly modeled oval face with tiny chin. The statue was carved from a single block of walnut and was

21. The Virgin enthroned. French (Burgundian), XII century

originally completely polychromed. The Virgin's gown and veil were green, bordered with vermilion, her hair was black, and her eyes were inlaid with blue enameled glass (only one eyeball remains).

In its severe frontality and its stylization of form and drapery, this statue is characteristic of the twelfth century, which thought of the Virgin as the "Throne of the new Solomon, incomparable, sublime, different from all thrones." This Virgin, however, is more than a traditional interpretation of Church dogma. She recalls the humble young Mary of the Annunciation and the mother who stood sorrowing at the foot of the cross.

STAINED GLASS, in fact glass of all kinds, was much rarer in the Middle Ages than is generally realized. The windows of chapels and small churches sometimes had panes made of translucent materials such as parchment, but more usually they were open during the daytime and covered only when the shutters were closed at night. Ordinarily, when the windows of medieval buildings (except cathedrals and great churches) were glazed, almost clear and usually diamond-shaped quarries were used. Most twelfth century glass has long since disappeared.

The two windows in the apse, at either side of the central window with grisaille, are composed of brilliantly colored panels believed to have come from a church in Troyes. They may represent Christ with an apostle, the Virgin and a monk (fig. 22), a bishop receiving a kneeling man, and a group of figures from an Adoration scene. This glass is of the type and quality of windows at Chartres and Bourges, and dates from the thirteenth century.

THE DOORS. The massive, ironbound plank doors at the entrance to the chapel are unusual both in size and in preservation. Such doors protected a church and its treasures from marauders and withstood all but the heaviest battering rams. As twelfth and

22. Stained glass. French, XIII century

thirteenth century doors usually received hard wear, they were replaced from time to time, a fact that in part accounts for the relatively small number of examples still in existence. The doors here
are probably of the twelfth century and are said to have come from
the Pyrenees region.

23. Capital from Langon. French, XII *century*

THE CHAPTER HOUSE
FROM PONTAUT

No ARCHITECTURAL UNIT could be more perfectly suited to
The Cloisters than the twelfth century chapter house (fig. 24) from
the former abbey of Notre-Dame-de-Pontaut in Gascony. The
chapter house is a complete architectural ensemble in the Romanesque style; both in period and in size it is well adapted to the adjacent
Cuxa Cloister. Stone for stone and brick for brick the room was
carefully taken down and re-erected here. Only the floors and
plaster vaults are restorations.

In every abbey the most important part, after the church, was
the chapter house where the monks assembled each morning to
discuss the business of the monastery. Sometimes the meeting place
of the chapter was an ordinary room, but often, particularly in the
late Middle Ages in England, a separate building was erected for
this purpose. The monks sat on benches around the walls. The abbot usually had a separate or a raised seat at the back of the room.
At Pontaut his seat may have been placed where a doorway (now
filled in) was later cut through the back wall when the room was
used for a stable.

The shape of the interior of the chapter house is irregular, the
corners not forming true right angles. The walls are not quite
parallel. The room measures 37 feet 8 inches along the cloister, 2
inches more on the opposite wall, and 25 feet 4 inches on the sides.
The two central columns supporting the round-arched ribs of the
vaults divide the ceiling into three bays. The west wall is pierced by
three windows, which were never glazed; there are hinges for

shutters and holes for iron bars. The carvings, moldings, and construction provide a lesson in medieval stonework. The varied decorations of the capitals (see fig. 26), the abaci, and the keystone bosses of the vaults include stars, rosettes, palmettes and other leaf forms, interlaced basket patterns, and confronted birds picking at grapes, pine cones, and an unidentified fruit. On the exterior the capitals are somewhat simpler in design.

In one wall and in some of the wall ribs (see fig. 25), brick supplements the soft yellow limestone. The style of the brickwork is consistent with that used elsewhere at Pontaut and recalls similar work, for instance that at Tournus, where brick was used even more extensively in combination with even less stone. The stone is thought to have been obtained at Dumes, beyond Hagetmau; probably because the builders had exhausted their supply of stone, locally baked bricks were used to complete the room.

Originally the walls were plastered, perhaps frescoed, and the ribs, as can be seen from traces of color here and there, were also painted. In the present installation it has seemed preferable not to attempt restoration of the stones and not to fill the joints completely. As the original floor tiles were missing when the room was acquired for The Cloisters, a twelfth century tile from the church at Cuxa was used as a model for the tiles manufactured for the present flooring; this has been inserted in the floor near the southwest window.

The few structures of this kind remaining in France, for instance those at Saint-Georges-de-Boscherville and Fontenay, are very similar to the Pontaut room; they usually open on the cloister walk with three large arches and are adjacent to the church of the monastery. At Pontaut the room was separated from the south transept of the church by the sacristy and the armarium, the library closet. The door originally leading to the sacristy has been walled

24. The Chapter House from Notre-Dame-de-Pontaut

25. Interior of the Chapter House from Pontaut

up and a new door leading from the Langon Chapel has been added. The dormitory was above the chapter room, as in most monasteries.

The abbey of Notre-Dame-de-Pontaut (also called Pontault, Ponteau, and Pons Altus) was founded by Geraldus, abbot of Dalon, about 1115. It was at first an abbey of the Benedictine order; but in 1151, in the time of Gaufredus, who had become its first abbot about 1125, the monastery was given to the Cistercians and placed under the rule of Pontigny. It was connected also with the abbey of Jouy, which was founded and favored by the kings of Navarre.

Notre-Dame-de-Pontaut was partly destroyed by the Huguenots in 1569; by 1572 only a priest, seven monks, and a wounded soldier were in residence there. In 1791, during the French Revolution, the buildings were sold to Dyzez de Samadet. His only daughter married a member of the Poudenx family who was related to the last abbot of Pontaut, and his brother was a deputy at the Convention and later a senator of the Empire. The structures that formerly belonged to one of the thriving monasteries of Europe are now dilapidated, and the place is rarely marked on any but the most detailed maps of the region.

The archives of the monastery have not been located, but the style of this chapter house and the armarium, sacristy, and the remains of some of the adjoining buildings suggest a date in the middle of the twelfth century for the early architecture. It is likely that the chapter house was built before the monastery became Cistercian in 1151, for after the *Apologia ad Guilelmum* of Saint Bernard (about 1127) the Cistercians tried to banish all sculpture from their churches and other buildings and thereafter had to depend for effect on purely architectural forms. The Romanesque Hall in The Cloisters, with its simple capitals and moldings, is reminiscent of the sturdy, severe Cistercian work found at Pontigny and related monasteries. Since the cloister at Pontaut, a portion of which has been reconstructed at The Toledo Museum of Art, was not built until the fifteenth century, it offers no clue to the dating of the chapter house.

26. Capital from Pontaut. French, XII century

THE CUXA CLOISTER

The ancient Benedictine monastery of Saint-Michel-de-Cuxa near Prades at the foot of Mount Canigou was in Romanesque times one of the most important abbeys of southern France and northern Spain. In the course of the eleventh and twelfth centuries, its fortunes guided by abbots as gifted in the arts as in monastic administration, Saint-Michel-de-Cuxa assumed a position of superiority over the religious and artistic life of what is now the province of Roussillon in France. Important elements of this abbey have been erected at The Cloisters (see figs. 27–32). Thirty-five capitals, nineteen abaci, of which two are decorated, seven arches, and part of the parapet coping come from the cloister. One capital comes from the tribune that spanned the nave of the church; two others, now flanking the Frías doorway, come from a large ciborium erected over the altar in the eleventh century.

Some of the capitals from the cloister are fashioned in the simplest block forms; others are carved with stout acanthus leaves or rinçeaux with a central motif of rosettes, pine cones, and heads of various types. The figurative capitals are cut in a wide variety of fanciful motifs: twin lions with single heads projecting at the corners, lions devouring humans or even their own forelegs, lions held by apes, humans grasping eagles by their necks, and fantastic heads atop palm trees. One capital in the east arcade, carved with mermaids holding their own tails, differs in technique and style from all the others. Its smaller dimensions, more delicate carving, the inlay of the eyes with metal plugs, and the use of the drill may be compared to similar features in five capitals still at Cuxa that probably supported the three arches of the tribune in the interior of the church.

The pairs of confronted eagles and animals must have been inspired, at least indirectly, by textiles and other objects of art from the Near East. Certain capitals may relate episodes taken from bestiaries or classical stories reminiscent of the fables attributed to Aesop. For others one is tempted to supply didactic meanings. Many of the motifs may once have been rooted in Christian themes of struggle between the forces of good and of evil, but in the Cuxa capitals the true meanings of these allusions have been lost, and the narrative image has become simply ornament of bold and vital strength.

All the capitals are vigorously carved; the planes are simple and clearly defined, creating a play of light and shadow. The architectonic arrangement of decorative motifs and figures gives strong support at the corners of the capitals for the abacus blocks above. Each decorative element is carefully built up upon the one below it, so that there is a unified structural transition from shaft to abacus.

The two large capitals of white marble placed on either side of the Frías doorway are no doubt from a ciborium. Documents tell us that in 1040 Abbot Oliva planned and erected a magnificent new altar and ciborium dedicated to Saint Michael; it is described in a contemporary letter by a monk called Garcia. It had a solid base symbolic of the strength of the evangelists in defense of the faith; four columns of pink marble, seven feet high, alluding to the blood of the martyrs; and four capitals in the Corinthian style, sculptured in white marble, signifying the candor and purity of spiritual gifts.

The reconstruction of the Cuxa Cloister is based on studies of the site, on evidence offered by original fragments, and on notes and drawings, some of them made in the nineteenth century by E. Viollet-le-Duc and J. Taylor, who saw the cloister before it was demolished. A plan of the monastery dated 1779 and excavations at the site concluded in 1953 indicate that the original Romanesque

27. Arcades and garden court of the Cuxa Cloister

cloister was roughly rectangular, 156 by 128 feet. Since not all its capitals are at The Cloisters, the reconstruction here is only a little over half the original size, being 89 by 78 feet, with walks twelve feet wide instead of fifteen. The original arcades were supported by fifty-eight columns and capitals, including two twin columns, and seven piers. At The Cloisters, corner piers similar to the original ones have been erected, but the intermediate ones omitted.

The antique portions of the Cuxa Cloister, beginning at the northeast corner, have been kept together wherever possible. When additional stone was needed to supplement the original elements, Languedoc marble was cut from the quarries between Ria and Villefranche that supplied the stone for Cuxa in the twelfth century. (The same mottled light red and gray stone, from the same quarries, was used for the decoration of the Grand Trianon at Versailles and for the mammoth columns of the Arc du Carrousel in Paris.) The floor tiles are patterned after old ones excavated from

28. East arcade of the Cuxa Cloister

the old walks at Cuxa. The timber roof, resting on stone corbels, and the roof tiles were suggested by precedents at Cuxa and elsewhere. In Mediterranean regions the process of making tiles has varied little since medieval times; the clays used and the shapes are the same, and baking processes are similar.

Saint-Michel-de-Cuxa was founded in 878 when the Benedictines abandoned the monastery of Saint-André-d'Exalada, in Haut Conflent, which had been destroyed by a disastrous flood the year before. At the suggestion of Charles the Bald, the abbot of Cuxa placed his "fifty monks and twenty servants, his already numerous lands, the thirty volumes of his library, and his five hundred sheep, fifty mares, forty pigs, two horses, five donkeys, twenty oxen, and one hundred other large animals with horns" under the protection of Count Miron, first of the counts of Conflent and Cerdagne. Under this auspicious patronage the monastery buildings were finished in 883.

The first church was replaced by a considerably larger one begun in 955 and consecrated in the presence of seven bishops in 974. At this time both church and monastery were dedicated to the archangel Michael, the favorite saint of a great patron of Cuxa, Count Séniofred of Cerdagne, as well as to Saint Germain, titular saint of the earlier church. In time, Saint Michael became the sole patron saint. Many relics were given the abbey during this period of enlargement and were placed in the altar of the church. Among them was wood from the Holy Manger, and so the abbey was called *monasterium proesepii Domini*.

The renown of Cuxa spread throughout Europe. Among the famous men who visited the monastery were Saint Peter Urseolus (the doge Pietro Orseolo of Venice), who joined the community as a novice, and two hermits, Marinus and Saint Romuald (Romualdo, a member of the ducal family of Ravenna and founder of the Camaldolese order). Oliva, abbot of Cuxa from 1008 to 1046, was a distinguished writer and poet and the most celebrated per-

29, 30. Capitals from Saint-Michel-de-Cuxa. French, XII *century*

sonality in southern France and northern Spain. Soon after his
election at Cuxa he also became abbot of Santa María de Ripoll
and bishop of Vich; he is said to have directed the construction of
the abbey church at Ripoll and the cathedral at Vich. At Cuxa his
chief architectural contributions were the ciborium erected in 1040
and the restoration of the church in which the fragments of the
Manger were preserved.

Although we do not know the precise date of the cloister at Cuxa
or the abbot responsible for its construction, it seems likely that it
was built shortly before the middle of the twelfth century, during
the tenure of Abbot Gregory. Certain nineteenth century records
mention a stone effigy in the cloister, inscribed to "Gregorius, abbot
and archbishop." Gregory, first mentioned in 1130 as abbot of
Cuxa, became archbishop of Tarragona in 1137, but he appears to
have remained at Cuxa, for he is mentioned as being there in a
document of 1144. His successor Josfred became abbot in 1145 and
Gregory is reported to have died in Tarragona the following year.
It is tempting to think that the monks placed their remembrance of

Gregory in the midst of architecture for which he was responsible. If indeed he was, the cloister and possibly the tribune would date within the years 1130–1145. Stylistically the Cuxa capitals and the carving of the tribune lend support to this date. They are closely related to similar elements at the nearby church of Serrabona, which was consecrated in 1151. If, on the other hand, the Cuxa cloister was built in the second half of the twelfth century it would presumably have been finished before 1188, for in that year began the administration of Abbot Arnald, who was so incompetent that he was deposed in 1203 by order of Innocent III.

The sacking of the monastery in 1654 by the troops of a local count, who had ordered the fortifications torn down, was the beginning of long years of despair. In 1791 the monks fled the abbey. The deserted buildings soon fell into complete disrepair; in 1835 the roof of the church collapsed and four years later the north bell tower crashed to the ground. Finally the monastery was sold in three parts to several inhabitants of the region. Ten of its arcades were removed to a bathing establishment at Prades and much of the remaining stonework was dispersed throughout the countryside.

31, 32. Capitals from Saint-Michel-de-Cuxa. French, XII century

Today the arcades from Prades and other scattered elements have been reassembled at Cuxa; they comprise a little less than half the original cloister. Parts of the tribune have been reconstructed as doorways; most of the other elements are at The Cloisters. A twelfth century marble fountain from the center of the cloister is at Eze-Village on the Riviera. Two capitals are in the Louvre, one in the Boston Museum of Fine Arts, and a fourth in the Pitcairn collection at Bryn Athyn, Pennsylvania. The fountain in the cloister of the Pennsylvania Museum of Art in Philadelphia is also said to be from Cuxa.

THE FRÍAS DOORWAY. A nineteenth century account of the church of San Vicente Mártir at Frías, near Burgos, describes in considerable detail the main portal, which was presumably made early in the thirteenth century at the order of Alfonso VIII, king of Castile from 1158 to 1214. A great fire swept the church in the sixteenth century, and when the tower fell in 1879 the portal was destroyed.

Eighty stones from this portal are incorporated in the reconstruction of the doorway in the north wall of the Cuxa Cloister. The reconstruction is based upon a study of the individual stones and related monuments in Spain. The problem of arranging these miscellaneous stone carvings as they would have been in the Middle Ages was doubly difficult because a number of stones had been used in an earlier construction and then had been reworked and used again. At the sides of the present installation two openings have been made so that the backs of some of these reworked stones can be seen.

The various voussoir blocks are like illustrations for a picture book, except that they are placed on a doorway, and those which are high up can scarcely be read. Some of the individual stones may be identified as follows. *Second arch from the outside* (beginning with the eighth stone from the right): a monk blessing a man starting on a journey; the monk wounded; the monk's deathbed; a wild rose; a woman, possibly symbolizing victory or courage, between two fighting warriors; a figure symbolizing lust; (on the last stone) two demons dragging a miser to hell. *Third arch* (beginning at the right): the Visitation and a seated male figure, possibly Zacharias; the Flight into Egypt; the devil tempting Christ to turn stones into bread; Christ raising Jairus's daughter; Christ sending forth the disciples to preach (?); Christ healing a dumb man; the Entry into Jerusalem (on two stones); Christ washing the feet of the disciples; the Last Supper (on two stones); the Betrayal.

THE NARBONNE ARCH. The twelfth century white marble arch over the doorway near the wall fountain is said to have

33. Manticore. Voussoir from the Narbonne arch. French, XII century

come from the former church of Saint-Cosmus at Narbonne; an
arch identical in style is now at the church of Saint-Paul-Serge at
Narbonne. The grotesque animals carved on the arch were often
represented in medieval bestiaries. Fom left to right they are: The
manticore (fig. 33), with the face of a man, body of a lion, and
tail of a scorpion—a horrible creature except for its flutelike voice.
The pelican, which kills her offspring, mourns them three days,
then revives them by pouring over them her own lifeblood (symbolic of Christ's sacrifice for mankind). The basilisk, so frightful
that it can kill man or beast merely by a look or a hiss but which is
itself killed by the weasel (symbolic of the fact that God made
nothing without a cure). The harpy, a birdlike creature with a
human head, which with its beautiful voice lures sailors to their
doom. The griffin, a winged animal which feasts upon humans. A
serpentlike creature which may be intended for a dragon or an
amphisbaena, a reptile with two heads. The centaur, with the body
of a horse and the arms and head of a man, a creature of great in-
telligence, yet ruled by animal passions. The lion, king of beasts,
who erases his footmarks with his tail when hunted (symbolic of
the Incarnation), sleeps with his eyes open (symbolic of the dual
nature of Christ on the cross), and brings to life his cubs, born dead,
by breathing on them for three days (symbolic of the Resurrection). Each animal is compactly designed to fill the space it occupies
on the voussoir, and all are expertly carved to form a richly patterned, harmonious whole.

FOUNTAINS AND LAVABO. The central fountain, possibly a font made into a fountain, comes from Saint-Genis-des-
Fontaines, and the wall fountain in a recess at the northeast corner
of the cloister wall, except for the two blocks supporting the basin,
is from the monastery of Notre-Dame-du-Vilar. The style of the
fountains is contemporary with that of the Cuxa capitals, and the
pink marble came from the same quarries. The stone slab placed

above the basin of the wall fountain and the basin itself were not used together when these two elements were found at Vilar, and an old photograph shows that the slab was at one time used as the tympanum of a doorway. But an examination of both elements, the two holes through which the water flowed, and parts of the doorway confirms the opinion that the slab and the basin formerly composed a fountain as they do now. The basin may have served as a reservoir from which buckets were filled or as a lavabo where the monks could wash their hands. Lavabos such as the thirteenth century Burgundian example in the southwest corner of the cloister had two basins, one for washing hands and the other for washing the Eucharistic vessels, which could be placed on the shelf above.

SAINT JAMES THE GREATER. The statue at the entrance to the Nine Heroes Tapestry Room is in the style of the great Claus Sluter, who created for his patron, Duke Philip of Burgundy, the so-called Well of Moses (1394–1404) for the Carthusian monastery of Champmol near Dijon. Sluter's conception of freely moving forms cloaked in yards of heavy, agitated drapery was an innovation. His influence was felt far beyond the borders of Burgundy and for many decades. Here Saint James with his pilgrim's hat and cockleshell is represented as a pilgrim to his own shrine in Compostela. The sculpture came from Poligny in Burgundy and is a companion piece to the Saint John the Baptist statue in the main building of the Metropolitan Museum. Originally these statues must have had gold over the entire surface, which was prepared with a red ocher underpaint. Only microscopic traces of the gold have survived.

THE NINE HEROES
TAPESTRY ROOM

THE THEME of the Nine Heroes—called in medieval English the Nine Worthies and in French *les Neuf Preux*—was developed and made popular about 1310 by a jongleur named Jacques de Longuyon in his *Vows of the Peacock (Les Voeux du paon)*. Porus, the hero of this courtly poem, fought "as never man had fought" before; he fought more bravely than even the nine great heroes of old. With the medieval poet's awareness of the symbolism of three and three times three, Jacques chose for his roster of heroes three pagans, three Hebrews, and three Christians. The pagans are Hector, Alexander, and Julius Caesar; the Hebrews, David, Joshua, and Judas Maccabeus; the Christians, Arthur, Charlemagne, and Godfrey of Bouillon. There were numerous representations of the Nine Heroes and their counterparts the Nine Heroines in fourteenth century sculpture, painting, manuscripts, and goldsmith work, and many great noblemen of the time owned sets of tapestries illustrating these subjects.

The only sets of fourteenth century tapestries of which substantial portions have survived are the Apocalypse tapestries at Angers and the Nine Heroes tapestries at The Cloisters.

The Cloisters set originally consisted of three tapestries, each more than 21 feet wide and about 16 feet high and each representing one of the three groups of heroes surrounded by smaller figures in an architectural setting. The set, like the Apocalypse tapestries, had been cut up and dispersed in the course of time. Nevertheless it was possible over a period of twenty years to assemble from four

34. Detail from the Hebrew heroes tapestry.
French, late XIV century. Workshop of Nicolas Bataille

different owners ninety-five fragments of various sizes and to piece them together to form more than two thirds of the original set.

Five of the heroes and almost all the accompanying figures have been recovered. The King Arthur tapestry was acquired by the Museum in 1932, when it was believed to be the only large fourteenth century piece we would ever have. Four years later a New York collector showed us packing cases containing five pairs of curtains made up of ninety-one pieces of fourteenth century tapestries that were immediately recognized as belonging to the same series. These fragments had been bought by Baron Arthur Schickler just after the Franco-Prussian War and made into window curtains for his castle at Martinvast near Cherbourg. Among them were three cardinals that originally surmounted the figure of King Arthur. Two figures cut from the right of the Hebrew heroes had been sewn to the left side of the Arthur at least as early as 1877, when the Arthur tapestry, thus composed, was lent to an exhibition in Lyon by Monsieur Chabrières-Arlès; these have now been properly placed in the Hebrew heroes tapestry. Another small figure in this tapestry had passed through many hands. Still another piece, the most recently acquired fragment, had been in a castle in Ireland, whither it had once come from Paris by way of London.

The most complete tapestry, on the north wall at The Cloisters, represents two Hebrew heroes with courtiers and warriors. The heroes are seated on Gothic thrones in elaborate Gothic niches; both are bearded and crowned. The figures are presented in contemporary medieval dress, with utter disregard for historical accuracy; even Joshua wears a crown. He is identified by the dragon on his shield and by the motif of the "sun in its glory" on the drapery beneath his feet. King David, with a golden harp, is in the center, and Judas Maccabeus would have occupied the place in the tapestry where a doorway now leads to the Cuxa Cloister. The little figures (see fig. 34)—spearmen and archers, courtiers and musicians—enliven the composition. A lady plays a rebec, another a

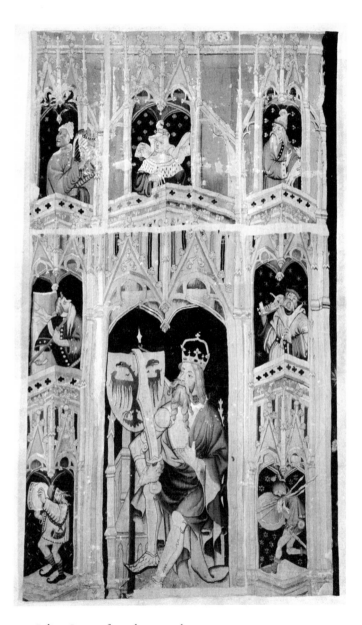

35. *Julius Caesar, from the pagan heroes tapestry*

harp, another a psaltery; one holds a cheetah, another a falcon, still another a tiny dog.

On the wall opposite, separated by a window with a fourteenth century stained glass panel, are the pagan heroes: Alexander the Great or Hector with a lion in a chair emblazoned on his shield, and Julius Caesar (fig. 35) with a double-headed imperial eagle in sable on gold; only the central figure is missing.

Of the three Christian heroes only the King Arthur (see fig. 36) has been found; Charlemagne and Godfrey of Bouillon have disappeared. Arthur is clearly identified by the three crowns representing England, Scotland, and Brittany on his surcoat and on his banner.

A recurrent detail in the Heroes tapestries at The Cloisters furnishes a clue to the identity of the original owner of the set. Ten of the fourteen banners flying from turrets in the Hebrew heroes tapestry (see fig. 34) and the escutcheons in the vaults above David and Joshua display the golden fleurs-de-lis of France on an azure ground within an indented border of red. Since these are the arms of Jean, duke of Berry, third son of King John II of France, it may be supposed that the set was made to Berry's order or woven for him as a gift.

With the exception of a set of Heroes tapestries woven with gold and silver threads, now lost, no similar tapestries are recorded in the inventories and account books of the duke. However, a series of Heroines, probably the companion set to the Cloisters Nine Heroes, is listed and described in an inventory of the possessions of Berry's nephew, Charles VI, made shortly before his death in 1422. The presence of the Berry arms on Charles's set suggests that these Heroines also belonged to Berry.

The Heroes tapestries may have been made for the Duke of Berry's palace at Bourges and may actually have been woven there. This possibility is suggested by an extract from a contemporary document which can no longer be found in the Bibliothèque Nationale but which was noted by A. de Champeaux and P. Gauchery

36. King Arthur. Detail from the Christian heroes tapestry

in their *Travaux d'art executés pour Jean de France, Duc de Berry* (Paris, 1894). According to this record there was a "payment made in 1385 to Jehan le Prestre, roofer and plasterer, for having completely reroofed the great hall of the palace at Bourges, where formerly the grain received as tithes by the duke had been kept and where *they were now making his tapestry* at the same time that they were cutting stones for the palace."

In the stained glass panels formerly in the Sainte Chapelle of the palace at Bourges there are elements that show, in both design and coloring, a relationship with the tapestries. The placing of large figures in niches and the silhouetting of some of the figures against Italian brocades are common to both. The architectural structures with groined vaults, the thin columnar sections supporting gables ornamented with crockets and finials, and the quatrefoil tracery below some of the figures are very similar. The tonality of the faces and hair is remarkably close. But even more striking is the similar use of yellow, outlined in red, for the crockets and finials of the architecture.

We know that most of the Angers Apocalypse tapestries were woven before 1384 for the Duke of Berry's brother Louis, duke of Anjou, by Nicolas Bataille, master tapestry weaver and merchant of Paris, who died about 1400. And we know that Berry also ordered textiles from Bataille. Payments to Bataille as early as 1374 are recorded in the voluminous but incomplete account books kept by Berry's treasurers, although the entries do not describe or itemize the purchases, merely noting their cost. The fact that Bataille's widow is listed among the creditors claiming settlements from the duke's estate in 1416 indicates that further orders were received from him.

The Apocalypse tapestries are the only woven pictures surviving that afford a suitable basis for comparison with the Heroes tapestries. During the loan exhibition of French tapestries held at the Metropolitan Museum in 1947–1948, pieces from both sets were

examined side by side. Both series are woven with double weft
threads and with approximately twelve and a half ribs, or warp
threads, to the inch. The same restricted colors, with similar shad-
ing in the same light and dark tones, appear in both sets. Shaded
reds and blues predominate, recurring at intervals in the pattern.
In both sets the stonework, woven in a golden tan color slightly
more faded in some places than in others, is silhouetted against a
very dark blue, almost black sky. The five heroes, like the large
Angers figures, are seated under vaulted architectural structures,
and such details as the butterflies and the foliage at the outer edges
of the tapestries are comparable. If the Heroes tapestries were not
woven in the same workshops as the Angers Apocalypse, they
must have been produced under virtually identical supervision and
by similarly trained weavers, before the end of the fourteenth
century.

THE EARLY GOTHIC HALL

The thirteenth century was one of the greatest artistic periods of the Middle Ages. It was during this time that Gothic architecture evolved from the early forms initiated by Abbot Suger at Saint-Denis into the unified and awe-inspiring style of the great cathedrals of Reims and Amiens. Thirteenth century artists also produced some of the most universal sculpture of all time—idealized, dignified, possessing the strength of Romanesque carving, yet imbued with a new grace and sensitivity. In the Early Gothic Hall and the Gothic Chapel are exhibited statues of both the thirteenth and fourteenth centuries that exemplify clearly the thirteenth century style and tendencies toward mannered elegance that occurred in the fourteenth.

THE SCULPTURES. The Virgin (fig. 37) from the thirteenth century choir screen of Strasbourg cathedral, one of the great monuments of the Middle Ages, is perhaps the most important early Gothic sculpture on this side of the Atlantic. The choir screen was constructed between 1247 and 1252, when it was recorded as in place. It was demolished, and its many sculptures dispersed, in 1680, as a result of the relocation of the altar required by changes in ritual in the time of Louis XIV. Fortunately the design of the original screen is preserved in a small drawing of about 1660.

In this drawing the Virgin is depicted as the fourth in a series of eight figures, mostly apostles, adorning the upper part of the screen façade. Originally there were two angels supporting the Virgin's veil, and two others flying above. The figure of the Child,

84

37. The Virgin from the choir screen of Strasbourg cathedral. French, 1247–1252

38. The Virgin and Child. French (Île-de-France), XIV *century*

the whereabouts of which is unknown today, was not shown sitting upon his mother's arm, but seated on a rosebush and offering what appears to be a fruit on which a bird is perched.

A comparison of the measurements, type of stone, and stylistic analogies with the other surviving choir-screen statues has made it possible to identify the Cloisters Virgin as the missing figure from Strasbourg.

With majestic yet simple grace the Virgin from Strasbourg expresses the most ideal and noble qualities of early Gothic sculpture. Unlike the rather austere and transcendental images of Romanesque times, such as the Autun Virgin in the Romanesque Chapel, this thirteenth century statue, while still very much the Queen of Heaven, seems at the same time more human and sympathetically aware of man's existence. The ample brow, almond-shaped eyes, small but firm mouth, and fine chin produce an idealized face which combines strength of character with gentleness.

The overshadowing veil emphasizes the delicacy of the features; the simple gown and the mantle of heavy material draped in angular folds contribute to the impression of dignity and strength that this figure conveys. The paint is original, having been miraculously preserved under coats of later repainting. The flesh tones, the gold of the cloak, and the blue of the gown so enliven this statue that it is hard to believe that it is carved in sandstone.

It is recorded that the Strasbourg Virgin was sold at public auction in 1913 for the sum of eighty-nine pounds and five shillings; for three decades thereafter it was in a private collection near Paris.

The imposing fourteenth century Virgin and Child (fig. 38) from the Île-de-France, the region around Paris, affords an excellent comparison with the thirteenth century Virgin from Strasbourg. Both are masterpieces of their time and both are excellently preserved, retaining most of their original paint. Both interpret the Virgin as Queen of Heaven, regal, gracious, and serene. The fourteenth century statue, however, is more relaxed; the figure swings in a graceful, balanced s-curve; the draperies are soft and pliant, revealing the form of the body beneath; the face is smilingly aloof.

This Virgin and Child, perhaps the finest of the fourteenth century statues from the Île-de-France, is in an extraordinary state of preservation. Only the scepter which the Virgin held in her right hand and the tips of her crown are missing.

A white veil bordered with narrow green and red lines is drawn over her golden hair. The Child clutches one end of the veil in his right hand and holds an apple in his left. His red tunic contrasts with the Virgin's, which was once gilded. Her blue mantle, lined with fur, is stenciled in gold to imitate brocade. The gold borders are studded with paste jewels.

For almost twenty years the statue was in the former Kaiser-Friedrich-Museum in Berlin. It was sold when that museum was negotiating the purchase of the major portion of the Guelph treasure. Previously it was in the collection of James Simon and Lord Caledon.

The Virgin and Child may be compared to the very similar but badly mutilated and weathered limestone statue to the right. The juxtaposition dramatizes how vital a part color played in medieval sculpture. Other fourteenth century French statues in this room show the s-curve and the pliant drapery characteristic of the period.

The limestone statue of a deacon holding a book in his left hand, originally with the palm of martyrdom in his right, is related in style to a group of apostles and saints formerly in the funerary chapel built before 1348 for the bishop of Rieux in Toulouse, and now in the Toulouse museum. The composure and serenity of this idealized figure sets it apart from the more dramatic religious sculptures typical of the fourteenth century.

The grandeur of the office of a bishop is strikingly represented in the standing figure raising his right hand in blessing (fig. 39).

39. Bishop.
  Italian, XIV century

40. Young King or Prince.
  Flemish, early XIV century

His chasuble is ornamented with a black orphrey decorated with quatrefoils. In one, God the Father is shown blessing; in those below, the letters of Ave Maria are placed against red backgrounds. This sculpture from the parish church of Monticchio, in the region of Aquila, is very similar to a well-known fourteenth century statue of a bishop in the Bargello in Florence. Both these figures are of wood, embellished with the care given to a panel painting.

The wooden statue of a young king or prince (fig. 40), poly-

41. *The Intercession of Christ and the Virgin.*
   Painting from the cathedral of Florence. Italian, about 1400

chromed and gilded, once belonged to the Grand Béguinage in
Ghent and may originally have been made for one of the two
churches within the walls of that community of lay sisters, or
béguines. Due to the absence of his arms and of attributes other than
the crown and princely robes, it is impossible to identify the figure
with certainty, but it seems probable that he represents the youngest
of the three Magi and was once part of an Adoration group. The
smiling, idealized face, the modeling of the curly hair, and the
simple treatment of drapery folds is typical of Flemish sculpture
of the first quarter of the fourteenth century. The squares of old
glass at the neckline of the gown are replacements made by the
Museum to approximate the jewels shown in old photographs of
the statue.

THE PAINTINGS. Over the lintel of the central doorway is
a fresco of Christ from a Florentine monastery that was razed to
make way for a street. The fresco may once have been used above
a door, as here, or as a lunette beneath an arch, possibly in a niche
above a tomb. It is by one of the followers of Nardo di Cione
(active about 1343, died in 1365 or 1366), to whom Ghiberti ascribed the frescoes in the Strozzi Chapel of Santa Maria Novella
in Florence. Some scholars attribute the fresco at The Cloisters to
Nardo's follower Niccolò di Tommaso.

The large, rectangular painting in tempera on canvas, a technique
unusual for this period, shows the Intercession of Christ and the
Virgin (fig. 41), and comes from the cathedral of Florence. Once
considered to be a processional banner, it is now acknowledged to
have been commissioned as an altarpiece for the cathedral. It has
been attributed to a late follower of Orcagna active in Florence
about 1400. The Virgin recommends eight small figures to Christ,
and the Italian inscription is translated, "Dearest Son, because of
the milk that I gave you have mercy on them." Christ in turn looks
up toward God the Father, and the inscription in translation reads,

"My Father, let those be saved for whom you wished that I suffer the Passion."

The tempera painting of the Adoration of the Shepherds (fig. 42) is probably from an altarpiece. Charming in composition and the handling of details and effective in coloring, this picture has a universal appeal. A product of the Sienese school of the middle of the fourteenth century, it is now ascribed to Bartolo di Fredi.

CEILING BEAMS AND WINDOWS. The wide arch at the south end of this gallery and the wooden beams of the ceiling, although of modern construction, were suggested by similar architectural components of early Gothic style in the reconstructed Salle des Chevaliers in the Porte Narbonnaise at Carcassonne in Toulouse. The imposing windows, however, are original elements of Gothic architecture. These windows are open and light, in contrast to the relatively narrow apertures piercing the thick walls of Romanesque buildings. They are pointed rather than semi-circular in form and are decorated by a series of interior traceries which not only gives support for the expanse of glass but also emphasizes the graceful vertical movement so characteristic of the Gothic style.

The three windows on the west wall came from Beaumont-le-Roger in Normandy. The fourth, placed between this gallery and the Gothic Chapel below, is of more intricate design and was formerly in the wall of the church at La Tricherie, near Châtellerault just north of Poitiers. All four date from the thirteenth century.

Here and there the larger windows have been repaired, but the original carving is readily distinguishable. The fine profiles of the moldings and the freehand cutting should be contrasted with the more mathematical and exact modern work in the Gothic Chapel. It is not the breaks and weatherworn surfaces that make authentic medieval architecture appear so vigorous and spontaneous but rather the straightforward design and sure execution.

42. *The Adoration of the Shepherds. Attributed to Bartolo di Fredi.*
Italian (Sienese), middle of the XIV *century*

THE GOTHIC CHAPEL

THE Gothic Chapel incorporates within its design features suggested by a small chapel in the church of Saint-Nazaire at Carcassonne and the church at Monsempron. This modern setting has been more completely developed than elsewhere in The Cloisters, in order to create an effective background for the objects exhibited. The capitals, however, are of the simple bell type, unornamented so as not to detract from the medieval stonework.

THE STAINED GLASS. The medieval stained glass panels have been supplemented by sections of modern glass which are an interpretation of the fourteenth century grisaille in the center window. Without some patterned background, the impression of light vibrating through semitransparent glass, so to be remembered in many European churches, would not have been obtained. Stained glass painted in grisaille was used early in the Middle Ages as a way of saving part of the great expense involved in filling vast windows with elaborately decorated glass. Especially in the north of France, where the light was not so brilliant as in southern districts, windows with the more transparent grisaille were sometimes preferred.

The lancet windows in this chapel were planned so that the two French stained glass panels with their contemporary grisaille could be placed in the apse. This glass is said to come from Évron, and on the basis of style it is dated in the first half of the fourteenth century. The figures closely resemble others in the cathedral of Évreux, which were made about 1330 and are universally considered to be among the finest examples of fourteenth century glass.

On the panel at the left the prophet Isaiah (YSAIAS), wearing a cap and a green mantle thrown over a reddish brown tunic, is silhouetted against a bright blue background. He holds with both hands a scroll bearing the inscription ECCE VIRGO, taken from the prophecy *Ecce virgo concipiet et pariet filium* (Behold, a virgin shall conceive, and bear a son. Isaiah 7:14) and frequently used in representations of him. On the other panel Saint Mary Magdalene is depicted with a red halo and draped in a red-brown cloak; her bare feet denote the penitent sinner. She holds her most usual attribute, an ointment jar. The saint is represented as weeping, with her head supported on her hand. This attitude of sorrow suggests the passage, "And they [the angels] say unto her, Woman, why weepest thou? She saith unto them, Because they have taken away my Lord, and I know not where they have laid him" (John 20:13).

The panel with Mary Magdalene bears the inscription M. MARTE. It would seem to have been partly restored at some time and a piece of old glass inscribed with the name of Martha, but from another window of the series, inserted. Or possibly the painter made an error and substituted MARTE for MAGDA. Martha was traditionally believed to be the sister of Mary Magdalene.

Stained glass which is brilliant in color, pleasant in subject matter, and careful in design is to be found in many small churches in Austria. It does not have the great vitality of much French glass, but it tells a story and is very decorative. The four panels inserted in the two other apse windows are Austrian work of about 1380. They represent Saint Bartholomew with knife and book, Saint John the Evangelist with chalice and serpent, and two scenes with Saint Martin dividing his cloak with a beggar.

Austrian panels of about the same period are inserted in the northwest window. The panel with the Virgin of the Mantle sheltering six figures, including a bishop and a king, in a mandorla supported by four angels, comes from the church at Maria Strassengel. The Annunciation and its associated canopy and the quatrefoil come from Ebreichsdorf, near Wiener Neustadt. The companion piece of this charming, colorful panel is in the Kunstgewerbe-museum in Vienna.

THE EFFIGY OF JEAN D'ALLUYE (fig. 43), of the thir-teenth century, comes from the abbey of la Clarté-Dieu, near Le Mans. It is a magnificent example of this type of sculpture and one of the few surviving in such fine condition. The figure is life-size and represents a young man, fully armed, lying with hands joined on his breast in an attitude of prayer. His feet rest against a small lion, symbolic of courage. In its conventional portrayal of the sub-ject as youthful and with wide-open eyes this effigy exemplifies the serenity of thirteenth century French sculpture.

Jean d'Alluye, Chevalier, seigneur of Châteaux (later, Château-la-Vallière), Saint-Christophe, Chenu, Noyant, Méon, etc., was the son of Hugues V d'Alluye and his wife, Guiburge de Chourses (Sourches). In 1240 he borrowed 150 livres tournois from the monks of the abbey of la Trinité at Vendôme to meet the expenses of a voyage to the Holy Land. In 1241, while in the East, he was given a relic of the True Cross by Thomas, bishop of Hierapetra. On his return to France in 1244 Jean d'Alluye gave the relic (now in the *hôpital* of Baugé) to the abbey of la Boissière. He died about 1248 and was buried in the abbey of la Clarté-Dieu, a monastery founded in 1239 and constructed on land in the parish of Saint-Paterne, over which Jean d'Alluye held seignorial rights. The tomb with the sepulchral effigy is said to have been erected in the church near the chapel of Saint Peter; on the wall behind the effigy was a bas-relief representing an abbot with several monks. According to another account, the tomb was in the cloister gallery near the en-trance to the church. That it was once in a niche can be determined by the carving.

THE TOMBS OF THE COUNTS OF URGEL. The four monumental Catalan tombs come from the Premonstratensian

43. Tomb effigy of Jean d'Alluye. French, XIII century

monastery of Santa María de Bellpuig de las Avellanas, north of Lérida in Spain. They were erected at the end of the thirteenth or early in the fourteenth century by Armengol X, count of Urgel (died 1314), in the Gothic church of las Avellanas, a monastery founded in 1146 (or 1166) by Armengol X's ancestors Armengol VII and his wife Doña Dulcia, as a burying place for themselves and their family.

The tomb of Armengol VII (fig. 44), originally in a niche in the presbyterium at the Epistle side of the main altar of the church, is the most elaborate of the Urgel monuments. Three lions support the sarcophagus, which is ornamented on the front with carvings in high relief of Christ enthroned in majesty and of the Twelve Apostles. An arcade of trifoliated, pointed arches frames the figures. In niches on the piers between the arches are small figures of angels and various saints. The ends of the sarcophagus are sculptured only in part, as the tomb was placed in a canopied niche from which it projected about half its depth. On the end at the spectator's right, two monks stand beneath a pointed arch that continues the arcade on the front of the sarcophagus. The arch is repeated on the corresponding end at the left, but the figures are omitted.

Armengol is represented lying full length on the sloping lid of the sarcophagus. His head rests upon two tasseled cushions, the upper one wrought with the arms of Urgel—checky, gold and black. Behind his head is an angel. His hands are crossed above his sheathed sword; a lion crouches at his feet. Behind the effigy and forming part of the same slab of stone are small figures of mourners, many rows deep. Standing in front are ladies draped in long cloaks and knights from whose shoulders hang swords; several couples on the left are seated. At the right, by the head of Armengol, is a cleric holding an open book; he is saying prayers for the dead. In the back rows are numerous figures wearing hooded mantles. Unfortunately, this part of the tomb has suffered serious injury, and few of the heads remain.

44. Tomb of Armengol VII. Spanish (Catalan), 1299–1314

Part of the funeral rites, the absolution, is represented on the superimposed panel, which is separated from the company of mourners by a molding ornamented with leaf motifs similar to those carved on the front of the slab near the head of the effigy. The figures in high relief carved on this upper panel are larger in scale than those on the sarcophagus. The central group has three figures: the celebrant and two clerics in dalmatics, who hold up a funeral pall in front of him. The celebrant wears the funeral cope; both his arms have been broken off, but there are indications that he probably held a crosier in his left hand; the right was raised in benediction or may have held the sprinkler for holy water. To the left of this group, a cleric assisted by a young server holds a vestment, probably the chasuble which the celebrant removes after the Requiem Mass. Next are a thurifer carrying a censer and an incense boat, and two assistants in copes. To the right of the central group are a deacon, a bearer of holy water (?), a thurifer, and three assistants in copes. In the background are other members of the clergy. Above the central group a small naked figure, representing the soul of the deceased, is borne to heaven by angels.

The effigy of Armengol VII is very similar to those of the other Avellanas tombs, and all may be the work of the same artist. The sarcophagus is related to the retable from Anglesola, now in the Boston museum, and to some sculptures in the not too distant cathedral of Tarragona. Various French sculptors, including at least one from Tournai, who are mentioned in contemporary texts as working in Catalonia, have been suggested as the link between the art of the north and these Spanish monuments which show strong northern influence. The Avellanas tombs are superior in quality to any of the somewhat later Catalan monuments inspired by the northern style and may be in part the work of northern artists.

In execution the relief with the celebrant is different from and inferior to the effigy and the sarcophagus of Armengol VII. The supporting lions are somewhat coarser, although perhaps more architectural in feeling, and were probably not made by the sculptor or sculptors who worked elsewhere on the tomb. Such sculptures as these lions occur again and again in tombs and sepulchral monuments throughout Catalonia during the fourteenth century. Reliefs very similar to the one with the celebrant are also found elsewhere. It is possible, even probable, that such less important parts were "carried in stock" or made to order at various places.

45. Double tomb of Armengol x and Doña Dulcia.
   Spanish (Catalan), 1299–1314

The assimilation of sculpture from different workshops would account for the use of stone from different quarries for the various parts of the same monument.

Armengol X erected on the opposite side of the church of las Avellanas a double tomb (fig. 45) for his own remains and those of Doña Dulcia, wife of Armengol VII. The tomb as shown at The Cloisters is supported by two simple blocks that are modern restorations after photographs of the originals, which have disappeared. The sarcophagus of Armengol X, placed above that of Doña Dulcia, bears the arms of Urgel; Doña Dulcia's displays the arms of Foix and Urgel. On the slanting lids of the sarcophagi are effigies, the heads reposing on tasseled cushions incised with the arms of the departed; an angel holds the pillow under Doña Dulcia's head. Armengol's feet rest on the back of a dog, symbol of fidelity and domesticity. Doña Dulcia's feet are placed as if she were standing; they are supported by a corbel with a protecting griffin carved on its underside.

The fourth tomb (fig. 46), originally in a niche in the side chapel of the church of las Avellanas, is that of Don Alvaro de Cabrera the Younger, brother of Armengol X. Don Alvaro was killed in the battle for Sicily in 1299, and in his effigy he is shown clad in full armor. A dog wearing a collar decorated with bells crouches at his feet. Two lions support the sarcophagus, on which are displayed the arms of Urgel.

Jaime (Jacobus) Caresmar, abbot of las Avellanas from 1766 until 1769 and a resident there from 1740 until his death in 1791, wrote a history of the monastery from its founding until 1330. In this work, based on original documents, he described the tombs in great detail. At the opening of Alvaro's tomb in 1739 an old parchment was found sewn to the linen cloth covering the bones; it stated that Alvaro's "spirit sought the stars in the year 1299" and that "Ermengaudus [Armengol] X, count of Urgel, set up this monument to his very dear and deserving brother."

*46. Tomb of Don Alvaro de Cabrera the Younger.
Spanish (Catalan), 1299–1314*

The monastery of las Avellanas passed into private ownership
as a result of the Spanish laws of 1835–1837 decreeing the sequestra-
tion of Church properties. In 1906 the tombs were sold and the
remains of the bodies were removed to the church of Vilanova de
la Sal, a town founded by Armengol VII and once owned by the
monastery of las Avellanas.

TOMB SLABS. By the thirteenth century the ever-increasing
number of sepulchral monuments had begun to crowd the churches
and chapels, and tomb slabs placed level with the floor were used
extensively to mark places of burial. These slabs, sometimes made
of metal but more frequently of stone, were at first unornamented
and bore only a simple inscription giving the name of the deceased,
the date of his death, and a conventional declaration of his virtues.
In time the slabs became more elaborate. The fourteenth century
tomb slab of Clément de Longroy and his wife Beatrice de Pons,

engraved in limestone and inlaid with white marble, is said to come from Aumale, near Dieppe. Clément is shown dressed in plate armor with a sword girded at his side; at his feet is a lion, and at either side of his head a shield emblazoned with his arms. His wife is portrayed in the costume of the day; at her feet are two small hounds. Her coat of arms is emblazoned at either side of her head. Parts of the Norman-French inscriptions may be translated as follows: "Here lies the noble man Messire Clément de Longroy, called . . . Christopher, Sire de Fontaines, Major-domo of the King . . . and of the Queen Blanche, who died in the year of grace one thousand—. Here lies the noble lady, Madame Beatrice de Pons, Dame de Fontaines, wife of the said . . . Christopher, who died in the year of grace one thousand—." The dates on this tomb slab were never completely inscribed, which suggests that the stone was cut before the death of either Clément or his wife.

OTHER SCULPTURES. The two over life-size sculptures of Saint Margaret and another saint (fig. 47), with their original canopies, are among the most grandiose and well preserved of monumental Gothic stone statues. They are carved in limestone. Removal of heavy coats of the later repaint that protected these figures has revealed their original polychromy. The colors—for example, the greens and reds richly bordered with gold, only traces of which remain—give an excellent impression of the original condition of medieval sculptures. Even the necklace of the smaller figure was delicately painted and gilded. The ridged eyebrows are accented with dark paint that contrasts with the tawny flesh color.

These statues may be attributed to the Catalan school and to the third decade of the fourteenth century on the basis of their relationship to the recumbent figure of Teresa de Moncada Cervera in the Provincial Museum of Lérida. This effigy is from one of the tombs of the early fourteenth century chapel of San Pedro in the Old Cathedral of Lérida, now largely destroyed. The treatment

47. Saint. Spanish (Catalan),
about 1330

48. Bishop. French (Burgundian),
early XIV century

of the hair, the folds of the Gothic draperies, the incised ornamentation of the borders of the garments, the modeling of the hands, the flat planes of the faces, and in particular the ridges of the eyebrows are characteristics common to the Moncada effigy and these two statues at The Cloisters. In some respects they recall the Avellanas tomb figures.

Notwithstanding its weathered surface, the monumental figure of a bishop (fig. 48) has lost none of the dignity and solemnity originally portrayed by the sculptor. Statues of this quality are rarely seen except in their original architectural settings. This sculpture was discovered in the thirties in a garden near Chablis. In many respects it resembles the figure of the patron saint on the trumeau of the north portal of the Burgundian church of Saint-Thibault, to which the date 1305–1310 has been assigned. The bishop, a contemporary work, also may have been placed on a trumeau at an entrance to a church.

Two angels, both of which originally held candlesticks, have been placed on the corbels at either side of the tomb of Armengol VII; the horsemen known to have been there in the fourteenth century have long since disappeared. These charming thirteenth century sculptures recall the angels of the Coronation of the Virgin in the central doorway of Reims cathedral, and, like the tomb of Armengol VII, they retain significant original polychromy. Formerly the angel at the left wore a green mantle with a red lining, fastened with a clasp over a gilded tunic. The hair was completely gilded, but only a few traces of the gold now remain over the brown underpaint. The flesh tints are particularly interesting, the red paint on the cheeks accentuating the angel's archaic smile.

THE BONNEFONT CLOISTER

M OST, if not all, of the capitals on the two sides of the Bonnefont Cloister (fig. 49), and similar ones placed in the adjacent Trie Cloister, come from the former abbey of Bonnefont-en-Comminges in southern France. All are carved in gray-white marble from the quarries of Saint-Béat.

The cloister enclosure at Bonnefont was approximately rectangular. To judge from the buildings and traces of foundations still visible, it measured, including the walks, about 109 by 78 feet. An account written by Alexandre du Mège in 1807 relates that the cloister was still standing with its four galleries and 128 shafts supporting capitals (one for each two shafts) whose ornaments imitated both plants of the region and plants having no recognizable prototypes in nature.

Twenty-one double capitals, selected for their similarity in size and for the interest of their decoration, are installed in the two sides of the Bonnefont Cloister (see explanatory labels in the cloister). Five others have been incorporated in the arcade in the north wall of the Trie Cloister. Where necessary, a few new bases were made to supplement the old ones. Some of the shafts are original; others were probably made some years ago for the reconstruction of part of the Bonnefont cloister at the Déaddé house at Saint-Gaudens. Later, when the house was demolished, several of the arcades were erected in the public gardens at Saint-Gaudens, and these have been faithfully reproduced at The Cloisters. A fragment of an arch, taken from a rough stone wall near the original cloister at Bonnefont and used as a model for the profiles and carving of the new arches, has been inserted in the second arch east of the Gothic Chapel.

The type of roof over the walks, with its beams and trusses, was

suggested by the timber holes in the wall still standing on one side
of the cloister at Bonnefont, and the treatment of the beams themselves is reminiscent of similar timberwork in the former cloister
at Marciac. Froidour, who described the cloister at Bonnefont in a
letter written in 1667, says that "all the columns are of marble and
the ceiling is of paneled oak." It is not unlikely that this ceiling was
added in the sixteenth century by Jean de Mauléon, bishop of
Comminges, who was commendatory abbot of Bonnefont.

The garden court of the Bonnefont Cloister (fig. 49), while not
an archaeological reconstruction or one based on any particular
prototype, was in a general way suggested by various examples depicted in paintings and related works of art.

Since all the archives of the abbey of Bonnefont were burned
during the French Revolution, there is no documentary evidence
for the dating of the cloister. Coats of arms, among them those of
the counts of Comminges and of Béarn, appear on some of the
capitals, but as these escutcheons do not establish the period of their
carving, the cloister can best be dated by comparing the capitals
with those of other monasteries.

The capitals (see fig. 50) can be divided into two groups according to the style of their decoration, one comprising the capitals
of simpler type, the other—which includes all the larger capitals—
those with more sophisticated ornament. The first group is identical in style with capitals from the cloister of the Jacobins in
Toulouse, whose conventual buildings were completed in 1310;
moreover, the arches of this cloister are like those used at Bonnefont-en-Comminges. The second group is identical in style with
the capitals of the large cloister of the convent of the Augustinians
at Toulouse (now the Musée des Beaux-Arts). This convent was
built between 1310 and 1341 by brothers of the Augustinian order.

The abbey of Bonnefont-en-Comminges was founded in 1136
by six monks from the Cistercian abbey of Morimond on the in-
vitation of Flandrine, widow of Geoffroi de Montpezat, and was

49. Garden court of the Bonnefont Cloister

50. Double capitals from Bonnefont-en-Comminges.
  French, late XIII-*early* XIV *century*

favored by Roger de Nur, bishop of Comminges. When the
monastery began to grow, the counts of Comminges became its
patrons, and until the middle of the fourteenth century they were
buried there. The chapel was built in the second half of the twelfth
century.

During the nineteenth century most of the architectural sculpture from Bonnefont was dispersed. In fact, today there is scarcely a
place of importance within twenty miles where there is not some
vestige of the once-celebrated monastery. A meandering, almost
impassable wagon road now leads to the site of the former monastic
buildings. Part of the largest one still standing is used by peasants
for their farmhouse. Unfortunately, the records of existing sculpture have not been kept with sufficient care to permit positive
statements as to the origin of individual pieces. A group of the
capitals in The Cloisters was taken from Bonnefont about 1850 to
Saint-Martin-sur-la-Noue, near Saint-Marcet, and was used to
ornament the façade and gallery of a country house.

THE TRIE CLOISTER

In 1571 the convent of Trie, not far from Toulouse, was destroyed, except for the church, by the Huguenots. Shortly afterward some of the sculptured white and gray-white capitals from the cloister, and probably some from the nearby cloister of the monastery at Larreule, were sold to the Benedictine monastery of Saint-Sever-de-Rustan for the rebuilding of its cloister, which had also been damaged by the Huguenots. The cloister at Larreule has long since disappeared; according to some of the villagers, most of the sculpture and architectural stonework was used for the construction of a dam. Forty-eight of the capitals from Saint-Sever-de-Rustan, twenty-eight of which came originally from Trie, were sold in 1889–1890 by the commune to the city of Tarbes, capital of the canton of Bigorre. Some of these were erected with their old arches and parapet copings in the Jardin Massey at Tarbes, where they are now preserved with pride. Others are in the United States.

Of the latter, twenty-three, eighteen of which are known to have come from Trie, are in The Cloisters. The capitals, several old bases, and a section of an arch from Larreule, whose moldings are identical with those of the arches in the Jardin Massey, have helped make possible a reconstruction of three sides of a cloister at Trie (see fig. 51; see explanatory labels in the cloister). The fragment from Larreule has been inserted in the first arch of the west arcade. On the fourth side capitals from Bonnefont have been used. The tiles, roof timbers, and ceiling were suggested by existing work of the period.

The capitals from the cloister at Trie are believed to have been carved between 1484 and 1490. The earlier date is established by the

seventh capital of the west arcade, which is carved with the arms of
Catherine, queen of Navarre and countess of Bigorre, quartering
the arms of her husband, Jean d'Albret. The capital would not have
been carved before the date of their marriage, June 14, 1484. The
date 1490 is determined by a capital, not in The Cloisters, bearing
an inscription referring to Pierre II, cardinal of Foix (died 1490),
as still living at the time the capital was executed.

Numerous coats of arms, perpetuating the names of local fam-
ilies, appear on the capitals. They are an indication of the increasing
secularization of the arts in the late Gothic period. Grotesque subjects were also freely used, but the usual scenes from the Bible and
legends of the saints predominate in the series. The historiated
capitals do not represent all the scenes which might be expected,
largely owing to the fact that of the eighty-one known to have
been at Trie, only eighteen have been gathered together here.

The capitals have been placed in the west, south, and east arcades
and have been arranged, wherever possible, according to the
chronological order of the scenes represented, beginning at the
northwest corner near the entrance from the Bonnefont Cloister.
The most important subjects depicted are as follows. *West arcade*:
first capital, God creating the sun, moon, and stars (a sundial was
at one time on the top face); second capital, the Creation of Adam,
arms of La Barthe-Fumel, the Creation of Eve; third capital, Abraham leading his son Isaac to the sacrifice, arms of Jean III, count of
Astarac, the Sacrifice of Isaac; fourth capital, arms possibly of
Algoursan, and the same arms quartered with unidentified arms;
fifth capital, armed boy and basilisk, Saint Matthew writing his
Gospel, with his symbol, an angel, and arms of La Roche-Fonte-
nilles; sixth capital, Saint John the Evangelist writing his Gospel,
with his symbol, an eagle, and two children probably spinning
tops with whips; seventh capital, arms of Catherine of Navarre
supported by a bishop and Saint Anthony (?), arms of Ossun, Saint
John the Baptist and a kneeling adorant, possibly Jean d'Albret,

51. Arcades and garden court of the Trie Cloister

52. The Nativity. Capital in the Trie Cloister.
French, probably about 1484–1490

husband of Catherine of Navarre; eighth capital, arms of Jean de Foix supported by John the Baptist and a female figure.

South arcade: first capital, the Annunciation to the Virgin Mary; second capital, the Nativity (fig. 52), the Annunciation to the Shepherds; third capital, the Massacre of the Innocents, the devil tempting Christ to turn stones into bread; fourth capital, unidentified arms; fifth capital, the burial of Lazarus, Martha and Christ, Christ raising Lazarus; sixth capital, Christ before Pilate, the Flagellation of Christ; seventh capital, the Entombment of Christ.

East arcade: first capital, an adoring monk and the Virgin; second capital, Pentecost, Saint George killing the dragon; third capital, arms of the town of Trie or of Jean de Trie, Saint Michael overcoming the devil; fourth capital, Saint Christopher holding the

Christ child, a bishop, shield bearing symbols of the Virgin Mary, the monk Arnaldus and the Virgin Mary; fifth capital, arms of France supported by angels, the Stoning of Saint Stephen; sixth capital, Saint Catherine and Saint Margaret, the Temptation of Saint Anthony; seventh capital, arms possibly of Arnaud d'Antin supported by a knight and a child with a hobbyhorse, the arms of Cardaillac; eighth capital, Saint Martin sharing his cloak with a beggar, a woman with a distaff.

THE FOUNTAIN in the garden is composed of two late fifteenth or early sixteenth century limestone parts. On the front of the cross there is a figure of Christ between Mary and John; on the back Saint Anne, with the Child on her right arm and the Virgin at her left, stands between unidentified saints. The octagonal section is ornamented with seven apostles and John the Baptist in traceried niches; its original lead pipes issued from decorative heads just as the replacements do now. The shaft between the antique elements is modern, and the pedestal, of cast stone, is copied from the original in the Glass Gallery.

THE GLASS GALLERY

THE Glass Gallery has been so named from the seventy-five roundels and panels of stained glass dating from the fifteenth to the early sixteenth century which have been set into the windows. The tapestries and the sculptures are about contemporary with the stained glass, and all are excellent examples of the late Gothic style and the late medieval point of view.

STAINED GLASS. Stained glass roundels were very popular during the fifteenth and sixteenth centuries, particularly in England, the Netherlands, Switzerland, and Germany. Although commonly they represented sacred subjects, the roundels were used extensively in secular buildings. It was customary to set them in leaded panes of clear glass.

53. The Adoration of the Magi and the Flagellation.
   Stained glass roundels. German, xv century

The characteristic bright yellow color was produced by a silver stain, which was fused on the outside of the glass. This technique afforded new possibilities in the manufacture of stained glass, for it permitted craftsmen to execute two-color cartoons without using as many leads as had formerly been required. At first a pale golden transparency was obtained, and subsequently many shades between light lemon yellow and deep amber. The dark lines on the roundels were drawn on the inner surfaces and then fired in a kiln; afterward details were sometimes accentuated, or patterns made, by scraping away portions of the opaque areas and exposing the glass.

The roundels show considerable variety in subject and in manner of presentation (see fig. 53). There are scenes from the life of Christ, his birth, passion, and resurrection; two of Christ's parables, the Prodigal Son and the Rich Man and Lazarus, are also illustrated. Among the Old Testament scenes are incidents from the story of Esther and Ahasuerus and of Joseph in Egypt. From the Old Testament Apocrypha comes the story of Tobit. Many of the roundels represent saints and others show coats of arms. As Gothic and Renaissance details often appear in a single panel, the dating of the roundels is exceedingly difficult. The style is often derived from manuscript illuminations and illustrations from printed books. Artists noted for their drawings and paintings are known to have furnished designs for stained glass.

In the large late Gothic window looking toward the Trie Cloister there are two stained glass panels showing the kneeling figures of Wilhelm von Weitingen and his wife, Barbara von Zimmern, with their coats of arms. Both panels have flashed blue backgrounds, one with holly and birds, the other with hopvine and birds. This glass, dated 1518, was presumably made for the church at Sulz am Neckar, where the donors lived. It is said to have been owned for seven generations by a family named Meebold, who acquired it when the church was restored in the seventeenth century.

THE HONOR TAPESTRY (fig. 54). The lady Honor with ermine-lined robe and flower-decked headdress is seated in a small garden against a grassy bench. In one hand she holds a rosebud, in the other a half-finished chaplet of flowers. Her cutting knife is thrust into the soft turf. On the banderole at her feet the inscription, translated, reads, "I am Honor who make chaplets for my children who are so beautiful." The other inscriptions have been inaccurately restored in certain passages; consequently an exact interpretation is not possible. The young girl at the right is probably saying, "To please my friend better, I shall put on this pretty hat." The speech of the gentleman at the left may be, "Homage to my good lady, my protectress." The courtier at the right identifies himself as Deduit, or Pleasure. It is possible that Deduit is meant

54. Honor tapestry. Flemish (Arras or Tournai), about 1430

to proclaim, "Pleasure am I who defend [Joy] and Lece [Mirth], well loved."

In the thirteenth century allegorical poem *The Romance of the Rose* Deduit is an important character and the lady Leece is his companion. Honor and Deduit appear together in the fourteenth century poem *Le Lay amoreux* by Eustache Deschamps (1346–1406), where Honor also makes chaplets of flowers. Joie, Honours, Deduit, and Leece are among the allegorical figures in Deschamps's *Lay de franchise*, honoring King Charles VI on the first of May.

The style of the costumes in the Cloisters tapestry, the boldness of the technique, the decorative patterning of the background indicate that it was woven about 1430 in one of the great northern tapestry centers, Arras or Tournai.

THE PIETÀ, LAMENTATION, AND ENTOMBMENT. The theme known as the Pietà—the Virgin Mary, seated alone, mourning over the dead body of her son—became a popular subject in the late Middle Ages, inspired partly by the teachings of the German mystics. An impressive Rhenish Pietà (fig. 55) produced in the third quarter of the fourteenth century treats the subject with dignity and restraint. The full folds of the Virgin's robe, its gold borders enriched with jewels, are in striking contrast to the flat modeling of the figure of Christ.

The Pietà was introduced into France from the Rhineland early in the fifteenth century. The French group in this gallery is distinguished by the aristocratic fineness of the Virgin's face, the graceful sway of her body, and the elegant sweep of the soft drapery folds of her gown. Though the statue was produced in the early fifteenth century, it recalls fourteenth century sculptures of the Île-de-France and Champagne. The smallness of Christ's body may reflect the writings of German mystics who believed that the Virgin, in the agony of her grief, imagined that she was holding her dead son as a child again in her arms.

55. The Pietà. Rhenish, 1350–1375

56. The Lamentation. Hispano-Flemish, about 1480–1500

57. Bishop with donor. French (Burgundian), 1450–1500

In contrast to the serenity of the Virgin in the French Pietà, two figures of holy women from an Entombment group display extreme emotion in their contorted bodies and tear-stained faces. These dramatic figures, carved between 1520 and 1530, derive from the famous atelier of the Saint Martha at Troyes, and represent the late Gothic style in Champagne. They are said to have been found embedded in a wall at Chartres.

The head of Christ crowned with thorns, carved in limestone, is executed with the sensitiveness characteristic of the school of Champagne, but the treatment is more restrained than in many other fifteenth century representations of the subject.

The sculptured altarpiece of the lamentation over the dead body of Christ (fig. 56) is one of the most poignant interpretations of this theme in medieval art. Here John the beloved disciple, Mary Magdalene, and two other holy women join the Virgin Mary in mourning the death of their master. Each person in the compactly organized group expresses his own particular grief; together they express the sorrow of the whole Christian world. The sculptor of the altarpiece was strongly influenced by Flemish painters, especially Rogier van der Weyden. Typically Spanish, however, are the gilded framework, the brocaded side walls, and the painting of the city of Jerusalem in the background. The altarpiece, which originally probably had painted wings, can be dated about 1480–1500.

SCULPTURES OF SAINTS. In the late Middle Ages sculpture became more realistic. Saints and other holy people took on the aspects of ordinary people on the streets of a town or in a castle or a cathedral.

The portly gentleman with a conspicuous paunch and a money pouch at his belt may have been intended to represent a saint, or more probably either Nicodemus or Joseph of Arimathea from an Entombment group; but he appears here as a wealthy burgher who enjoyed good living. This impressive fifteenth century figure carved in limestone is in the Burgundian style.

Also in the Burgundian style is the polychromed statue of a bishop with donor (fig. 57). The inscription on the base may be translated as, "H. Cordier. Saint Germain, pray for us." H. Cordier is probably the name of the kneeling donor. The saint is either the fifth century bishop of Auxerre or the sixth century bishop of Paris, both of whom were named Germain. The statue was found in the town of Poligny and is very similar to a statue of Saint Nicholas in the parish church of Moutiers-Saint-Jean. It dates in the second half of the fifteenth century.

The small figure with uplifted hand represents Saint Francis receiving the stigmata. Dressed in his friar's robes and with tonsured head, he presents a countenance as individualized and expressive as a portrait in a Flemish painting. This limestone statuette, dating from the fifteenth century, was found on a roadside near Beaune in Burgundy.

Saint Barbara (fig. 58) is a very demure, very young French maiden of noble family, gowned in blue with silver patterns and wearing a chaplet of flowers in her thick golden hair. Only her attribute, the tower in which she was imprisoned by her father, indicates that she was a saint. The statue is north French, about 1500.

The rather haughty lady with a book in her hand (fig. 59) may be Saint Catherine of Alexandria, who was famed for her learning. She appears here as a wealthy bourgeoise, dressed in a red gown that was once brocaded and a gold cloak lined with brocaded material in silver and black. Her jeweled "pony tail" coiffure and slit sleeves were Italian fashions introduced into the north in the late fifteenth century. This remarkable statue, carved of linden wood and magnificently polychromed, was undoubtedly part of an altarpiece and was probably made in the upper or middle Rhine Valley about the year 1510.

The recumbent figure represents Saint Anne with her newborn

58. Saint Barbara.
    French, about 1500

59. Saint.
    Probably Rhenish, about 1510

daughter, the Virgin Mary, wrapped in swaddling clothes. In the tenderness of her gaze and the gentleness of her touch Saint Anne is a very human mother. Two areas of rough unpainted wood below and on either side of the infant Mary indicate that additional figures, probably angels, once attended the group. Many candle burns testify to the devotion with which this sculpture was regarded. Until 1885 the statue was part of an altarpiece dedicated to Saint Anne in the parish church of Ebern near Bamberg. In 1913 it was purchased by the Landesmuseum in Darmstadt, where it remained until 1937. This typically Franconian sculpture, dating about 1480, is remarkable for the condition of its paint.

A painted and gilded relief, carved in stone pine, probably represents Saint Lawrence presenting the poor as the true treasures of the Church. Possibly from the same altarpiece come reliefs of Saint Lawrence's martrydom in the Landesmuseum in Innsbruck, Austria, and Saint Lawrence with Pope Sixtus in the Bavarian National Museum of Munich. These sculptures are attributed to a follower of Michael Pacher working in Bruneck in the Tyrol; they date about 1490.

A limestone relief presents the incident from the life of Saint Hubert when he went hunting on a day in Holy Week and encountered a stag bearing a crucifix between its antlers. This early sixteenth century sculpture is said to have come from Burgundy.

THE ABBEVILLE WOODWORK (fig. 60). In the north of Europe, where wood was plentiful, it was employed extensively for building, often in combination with stucco. The elaborately carved woodwork adjacent to the staircase came from the courtyard of a house at Abbeville known as the House of Francis I, although it was probably built in the reign of his predecessor, Louis XII (1498–1515). The door at the right originally opened on a spiral staircase which led to the second floor. The small figures on brackets represent Saint Catherine, an apostle, and prophets. The initials on the panels have not been identified.

60. Woodwork from Abbeville. French, late xv–*early* xvi *century*

61. Wrought iron mounting. French, XI–XII *century*

THE TREASURY

THREE ROOMS have been set apart at The Cloisters as the Treasury; in them are shown objects of exceptional quality, some of which come from the Hermitage in Russia and from great art collections in Paris.

As early as the time of the Emperor Constantine, gold and precious materials were collected for the fashioning of sacred vessels; the kings of France, in the sixth and seventh centuries, enriched the abbeys of Saint-Germain-des-Prés and Saint-Denis. As such

128

possessions accumulated, abbeys and monasteries, cathedrals and churches, kings and nobles formed treasuries where valued objects used for religious services and state occasions were placed for safe-keeping. Sometimes church treasures were locked away in the crypt, but more generally they were placed in stout cupboards or in the thick walls of the sacristy, where the treasurer, who usually slept there, could guard them. Some treasures were kept continuously on view for the faithful in the sanctuary; others were exhibited to the public only at long intervals.

Anteroom

THE WROUGHT IRON MOUNTINGS (fig. 61) on the modern oak doors at the entrance to the Treasury were made for a church door at Saint-Léonard-de-Noblac in the south of France. They have been dated eleventh or twelfth century and compare

62. *The Nativity and the Vision of the Magi. Detail from an altarpiece by a follower of Rogier van der Weyden. Second half of the xv century*

closely to decorative motifs in eleventh century manuscript illuminations of the region, particularly two from the nearby monastery of Saint-Martial in Limoges.

THE PAINTED ALTARPIECE has as its central theme the Nativity (fig. 62) with God the Father above, surrounded by jubilant angels. On the left is the Vision of the Emperor Augustus, on the right the Vision of the Magi—both described in *The Golden Legend*, the lives of the saints, by Jacobus da Voragine. In the first of these scenes the Tiburtine Sibyl answers Augustus's question whether there was anyone alive as great as he by showing him a vision she beholds in the center of the noonday sun, a maiden holding a child in her arms. In the other scene the Magi, after bathing and praying, behold in a star the Child, who directs them to Jerusalem where they will "find the son of the Virgin, God and Man, which was then born." The Visitation and the Adoration of the Magi are shown on the wings. The figures on the reverse of the wings, Adam and Eve and Saints John the Baptist and Catherine of Alexandria, are not visible when the retable is open.

This altarpiece was once in a convent in Segovia. Even though it lacks the original framework and two lower wings, it is extraordinarily well preserved. In large part it was inspired by Rogier van der Weyden's similar altarpiece, commissioned about 1445 by Peter Bladelin, treasurer of the Duke of Burgundy, for the main altar of a church and now owned by the Berlin-Dahlem-Museum (formerly the Kaiser-Friedrich-Museum) in Berlin.

THE WOOD PANELING. Thirty-seven elaborately carved oak panels representing scenes from the lives of the Virgin and of Christ (see fig. 63) have been set in the modern wainscoting. They are said to have been made about 1500 for the royal abbey of Jumièges in Normandy, perhaps to decorate the choir stalls ordered by the abbot Jacques d'Amboise in 1501 or panels of the choir

63. *The Massacre of the Innocents and the Flight into Egypt. Wood panels. Franco-Flemish, early* XVI *century*

screen erected during his administration (1471–1504). The differing figure styles and the various treatments of the rich architectural ornament above each scene indicate that they are the combined product of at least four master craftsmen who worked with the skill for which wood carvers from Flanders and this region of France were famous. The rich furnishings of the abbey of Jumièges were dispersed after the French Revolution and the panels here may have been sold at that time. Early in the nineteenth century they were brought by the British Ambassador to France, Lord Stuart de Rothesay, to Highcliffe Castle in Hampshire, England, where they remained until 1950.

THE ANGELS placed above the door, playing a rebec and a lute respectively, are charming small sculptures made in south Germany around the year 1500. Angels similar to these are to be found in a number of carved altarpieces of the late Gothic period.

First Room

THE CHALICE OF ANTIOCH (fig. 64), made in the early Christian era for use in the sacrament of the Lord's Supper, is said to have been discovered in 1910 by Arabs digging a well near Antioch, one of the important early centers of Christendom in the East. The chalice is composed of two cups: an undecorated inner one of silver set into an outer cup. The latter is decorated with silver openwork enriched with gilding, and cast in a series of grapevines in which appear birds, animals, and insects. The grapevines encircle twelve male figures—ten apostles and two representations of Christ.

This cup, one of several historic and distinguished liturgical chalices at The Cloisters, is probably the earliest known surviving Christian chalice. It has been the subject of a vast literature, partly

owing to an early thesis that the inner cup is none other than the
Holy Grail used at the Last Supper. Although today scholars do
not accept such an early date, there is as yet no universal agreement
on an alternative date for the Antioch chalice. Most probably the
cup was created in the late fourth or early fifth century during a
period known as the Theodosian Revival. Another theory is that

64. The Chalice of Antioch. Early Christian, IV–VI century

the chalice is a product of the revival under the Emperor Justinian which occurred in the first half of the sixth century when the classical elements of the Theodosian style became blended with the hardness and abstraction of forms that had become prevalent during the course of the fifth century.

THE BERTINUS CHALICE (fig. 65), a sturdy sacramental cup, was hammered from heavy silver, and the interior and rim were gilded so that after cleaning no drop of consecrated wine would remain and the precious metals would glisten like new. The pierced knob with fantastic animals and foliage allowed for a good grip and concealed the fastenings of the cup to the well-proportioned base. The piece is a rare example of signed and dated silversmith work of the period. The inscription cut in the silver-gilt band around the bottom of the base, AD HONOREM B MARIE VIRGINIS F BERTINUS ME FECIT A° MCCXXII, states that the chalice was made by Brother Bertinus in 1222. Its place of origin, however, has not been established. A similar though smaller chalice in the Louvre, inscribed *Pelagius*, is thought to be Spanish because the name Pelayo occurs in northern Spain. The fact that there was a great abbey dedicated to Saint Bertinus near Saint-Omer in northern France might suggest that general region for its manufacture; also the style of the foliage leads to certain comparisons with work from the valley of the Meuse. Related works have also been found in England, Iceland, and Scandinavia.

THE CHALICE, PATEN, AND STRAWS. This elaborate and rare early Gothic chalice, together with the paten for the sacramental bread and straws for the sacramental wine, was purchased by Czar Alexander III in 1884 with the Basilewski collection in Paris and until the 1930s was one of the treasures of the Hermitage. The set was made in the second quarter of the thirteenth century in Freiburg in Breisgau for the nearby abbey of

65. Chalice by Brother Bertinus, dated 1222

Saint Trudpert. Saint Trudpert, a local saint, is portrayed below the figure of Christ on the paten. Around the bowl of the richly decorated chalice are Christ and the Twelve Apostles in niello, a compound of silver and sulphur that becomes a deep, lustrous black after firing and contrasts with the brightly polished metal. On the knob are four scenes from the New Testament and on the foot the four Old Testament scenes that prefigure them, all fashioned of gilt silver openwork stamped in relief, typical of upper Rhenish technique. The inscriptions and some of the figures are engraved and the lines filled with niello. The chalice and the paten are set with various gems, among them amethysts, sapphires, turquoises, and garnets.

THE BOWL FROM A CIBORIUM (fig. 66). In his *Treatise upon the Various Arts* the monk Theophilus, whose tenth or eleventh century manuscript was widely copied, described the techniques for working gold, silver, copper, iron, stone, and wood that were followed in "industrious" Germany, as well as the practices current in Italy, France, and Arabia. Niello, whose use he favored, is deftly combined with silver, parcel-gilt, in the ornamentation of a bowl, all that remains of a twelfth century ciborium, made to hold the consecrated Host. The human figures and fantastic animals, the heads of which are in relief, the foliage and the conventionalized designs are delineated with flowing calligraphic lines. The decoration suggests works of art made in various centers in England or on the Continent close to the English Channel, and thus the term Channel School has often been used to describe the general style.

The bowl was purchased by Alexander Basilewski in the nineteenth century in Novgorod and in 1884 was bought by the Czar for the Hermitage. A chalice of similar style and technique in the Stockholm museum was discovered by ditchdiggers in a pasture in Dune, Gotland. The export of such European wares to the east

and to the north from the eleventh century onward was part of a
general trade revival, chiefly among cities belonging to the Hanse-
atic League. Novgorod imported metalwork from the west in the
twelfth and thirteenth centuries. Gotland established trading rights
with Novgorod in 1229, with England in 1237.

66. Bowl from a ciborium. Channel School, XII century

THE FLABELLUM, or round liturgical fan, decorated with
silver-gilt filigree set with jewels, strips of highly polished tin,
enamels, and gilt bronze, derives from the feather and parchment
fans used in early medieval times "to keep away the small animals
that fly about, that they may not come near the cups" during the
Mass. In this form, however, the flabellum was probably more
ceremonial than functional and was placed on the altar or carried
in processions like a cross (the filigree panels of the inner band are
cruciform). Manuscript illuminations indicate that flabella were
usually carried in pairs. This one was formerly one of a pair in the

Hermitage in Leningrad. It was sold out of Russia in the 1930s and its companion piece remains in Leningrad.

It is difficult to be precise as to the date and place of origin of this spectacular piece. Certain of its elements relate to goldsmith work made around 1200 in Rhenish centers or in workshops of the Mosan region for export to the Rhineland. The foliated decoration of the outer band has, for example, a stylistic affinity to the cresting on the famous Shrine of the Three Kings in Cologne cathedral, but the enamels and the long strips of silver-gilt filigree appear in objects made around 1230 in the north of France under strong Mosan influence. The central boss of the flabellum is hinged and once contained a relic: the piece served as both ceremonial fan and reliquary.

RELIQUARIES. The cult of sacred relics was an important part of Christian worship as early as the fourth century when the Church first promulgated the doctrine that remains of martyrs and objects associated with Christ, the Virgin, and the saints possessed miraculous powers. In the later Middle Ages churches, monasteries, and even private individuals accumulated large collections of relics. Pilgrims traveled the length and breadth of the Christian world to visit the shrines where they were kept. As the theological importance of relics increased, so did the desire to put them into protective containers. The inscriptions, the illustrations, or the shapes of these indicated the nature of the relics they held; their physical beauty enhanced the spiritual significance of the venerated objects. Thus reliquaries are among the richest and the most imaginative of all church treasures. The earliest are simple boxes or caskets. Later examples may be complex architectural forms, statuettes, or shapes resembling the actual relics enshrined. Those at The Cloisters held no relics when they were purchased and are now of interest purely as works of art.

In the twelfth and thirteenth centuries the region of the Meuse

67. Reliquary statuette of Saint Stephen. Mosan, early XIII *century*

Valley in the medieval duchy of Lorraine produced goldsmiths and enamelers of such high achievement that their work was in demand throughout western Europe. The reliquary statuette of Saint Stephen (fig. 67) is one of the most important monuments of Mosan goldsmith work in this country. The silver-gilt figure recalls in technique the large gilded figures on the shrine of Our Lady in Tournai by Nicholas of Verdun, dated 1205. In his pose and in the youthful idealism of his face he reflects the influence of French cathedral sculpture that penetrated the region of the Meuse during

68. *Figure ringing hand bells. Detail from arm reliquary. Mosan, early* XIII *century*

the first quarter of the thirteenth century. The statuette probably once held a jeweled book, as do the statues of Saint Stephen at Sens and Chartres, containing the relic. On the reverse of the copper-gilt plaque is a vigorous engraving showing the Stoning of Stephen; above him is Christ in heaven, with two angels, one of whom bears in his arms the soul of the saint wearing a martyr's crown. The drawing is close to the work of Nicholas of Verdun and his school. The reliquary, formerly in the collection of the Duke of Arenberg, is said to have come from near Namur.

The arm reliquary (see fig. 68) once contained parts of the arm bone of an unidentified saint. It is made of silver plates, parcel-gilt, laid over an oak core and decorated by fourteen panels of rich filigree clustered around semiprecious gems, and fifteen plaques of niello depicting a variety of ornamental and figurative subjects. Near the cuff, on opposite sides of the arm, are Peter and Paul. A plaque just above the base has an animated figure energetically ringing hand bells. The goldsmith work of this reliquary reflects the style of a number of fine objects made in the early decades of the thirteenth century in the valleys of the Sambre and Meuse rivers. The niello work is related to the products of Brother Hugo, a renowned artist from the monastery of Oignies in the Mosan area. It is particularly close to that on a cover of an evangeliary in Namur dated 1228 and inscribed, "Some extol Christ by words, Hugo by his works in gold."

The shoe reliquary of *cuir bouilli* (boiled leather) was probably a protective and ornamental case for a metal receptacle that may once have contained a bone of the right foot of Saint Margaret of Antioch. Eight scenes embossed and tooled in the leather illustrate episodes from her life. A reliquary in the shape of the right shoe is fully appropriate for Saint Margaret, for a thirteenth century story of her life relates that when she caught the devil, who had come to deceive her, she threw him to the ground and "set her right foot on his neck, saying: Lie still, thou fiend under the foot of a woman." As only slight traces of paint remain on the four coats of arms, they have not been identified. By its style, however, one can tentatively assign this extraordinary piece (formerly in the Figdor collection in Vienna) to a French workshop of the mid-fourteenth century.

The tower reliquary, used for the display of the Host or for a relic, is an excellent example of the architectural type of shrine. Towers, crenellations, crockets, and finials, some decorated with minute gargoyles, enclose a rock crystal container topped by a tall Gothic spire. The style of the silver-gilt work and of the enamels on the base serves to place and date this piece in north Italy about 1400.

69, 70. Eucharistic dove and altar cruet. French (Limoges), XIII *century*

LIMOGES ENAMELS. In the twelfth and especially in the thirteenth century the production of enamel and copper-gilt work in Limoges in France attained the proportions of an industry. Copper was available only a few miles from the city.

The Eucharistic dove (fig. 69), symbol of the Holy Ghost, was suspended above the altar and used for keeping the Host in reserve. An unusual feature of this example is the movable wings.

Altar cruets were made in pairs for the Mass, one for water, one for wine. The enameled cruet shown here (fig. 70) is one of seven such cruets known to exist today.

Pairs of basins, one of which had a spout, were used for washing at mealtime. They are called gemellions, from the Latin word meaning twin. The spouted basin is decorated with a coronation scene surrounded by merrymakers; the other basin shows a knight on horseback surrounded by knights on foot.

BRONZES. No group of medieval bronzes is more fascinating than the containers for water known as aquamaniles (see fig. 71). An inventory of about 1150 for the treasury of Mainz cathedral describes "ewers of various shapes, called *manilia* because water is poured from them on the hands of the priests. Some have the shape of lions, others of dragons, birds, griffins, and other animals." To what extent the animals were symbolic and how widely aquama- niles were used for domestic purposes is not certain. Medieval

71. Aquamanile. German, XII or XIII century

bronze workers were adept in casting and refinishing various metals, using their mediums boldly. The combination of zinc with copper made a readily workable alloy. Like modern brass, this so-called *auricalcum* glistens like gold when it is polished. Though it has not been customary in museums to clean medieval bronzes, those at The Cloisters have been restored as nearly as possible to their original condition. To avoid further tarnishing and the need for constant polishing, they have been given a preservative coating.

72. Clasp of gilt bronze. Mosan, about 1200

The clasp of gilt bronze (fig. 72) was surely made in the region of the Meuse about 1200, although, curiously enough, a silver-gilt buckle identical in style was found at Dune in Gotland. The clasp may reflect the text, "Thou shalt tread upon the lion and adder: the young lion and the dragon shalt thou trample under feet" (Psalm 91:13). A few of these small objects are of such masterful execution

73. Bird. German or Italian, about 1200

that enlarged photographs of them reveal the plastic qualities of fine monumental sculpture.

The bronze bird (fig. 73), originally gilded, was found in Italy in 1925. It has been published as an imperial eagle made to surmount the staff of Frederick II, Holy Roman emperor and king of Germany, Naples, and Sicily, but it more closely resembles a falcon, possibly a gerfalcon, the falcon of kings. Frederick, who established his court in Naples in 1220, was an enthusiastic falconer and wrote the standard medieval text on falconry. However tempting it may be to associate this bird with Frederick or with one of his predecessors who are known to have held staves with eagles, the possibility that it was part of some architectural monument or a furniture mount cannot be discounted. In style the bird compares closely to those on various capitals of the cloister of Monreale cathedral, which is dated around 1200.

COVERED BEAKERS. In the later Middle Ages the increasing prosperity of the merchants permitted them to vie with the nobility in the luxury of their daily life and the lavishness of their gifts to the Church.

Two sumptuous covered beakers (see fig. 74) were probably made as presentation cups for the town hall of Ingolstadt, north of Munich, about 1470 by Hans Greiff, the town's leading goldsmith. An enamel plaque bearing the coat of arms of the city is fastened to the interior of the cover of the engraved beaker; the other has an Ingolstadt hallmark. Both were sold after the Napoleonic Wars; by 1863 the engraved beaker was in the possession of a local druggist, and the other also was privately owned in Ingolstadt. Both were acquired later in the nineteenth century by the Frankfurt collector Carl von Rothschild.

These silver cups, parcel-gilt, were once even more elaborate when all the beads, enameling, and paint were intact. Supporting the simpler of the two beakers are three armored knights holding

74. Covered beaker. German (Ingolstadt), about 1470

painted shields with bearded heads (restored), the arms of Burgo-
master Hans Glätzle of Ingolstadt. His portrait head above a modern helmet surmounts the finial. The shields of the engraved cup,
held by "wild men," are bare, but were probably painted with the
donor's arms. The foliate finial was originally entirely painted and
enameled in naturalistic colors. The deep engraving recalls the style
of the prints of the Master E. S.

THE MONKEY CUP (see fig. 75), a rare beaker of silver and
silver-gilt, is decorated in painted enamel with mischievous monkeys who have robbed a sleeping peddler of his clothes and his
wares and are making merry with them. On the inside of the cup
two other monkeys are hunting stags in a forest of beautifully
stylized trees. It is believed that the beaker was made about 1460 by
Flemish or Franco-Flemish artists for the Burgundian court. An
enameled spoon in the Victoria and Albert Museum showing a

75. *Monkeys robbing a sleeping peddler.*
    Detail from the "monkey cup." French (Burgundian), about 1460

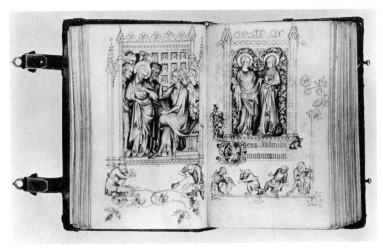

*76. The Book of Hours of Queen Jeanne d'Évreux,
illuminated by Jean Pucelle. French, 1325–1328*

monkey riding a stag is similar in technique and design and may
have belonged to the same set. The "monkey cup" has been in
many great collections including those of the Earl of Arundel and
J. Pierpont Morgan.

BOOKS OF HOURS. In the fourteenth and fifteenth centuries an increasing number of works of art were commissioned by
individuals for their private devotions. Among these were the
Books of Hours, abbreviated versions of the service books used by
the clergy. They include prayers and readings arranged according
to the eight canonical hours of the day, matins through compline;
hence their name.

The *Hours of Jeanne d'Évreux* (see fig. 76) has been identified with
"a very little book of prayers" given to Jeanne d'Évreux by her
husband, King Charles IV of France, sometime between 1325
when they were married and 1328 when the king died. A crowned
queen is twice shown at prayer in miniatures in the manuscript.

Jeanne's will specifically states that the "very little book" was illuminated by Pucelle.

Jean Pucelle was an illuminator in Paris, active at least from 1319 to 1327. Two manuscripts that bear his name and those of his collaborators are valued possessions of the Bibliothèque Nationale in Paris. The uniform excellence of every single page in the book at The Cloisters indicates that Pucelle undertook the whole work himself. There are full-page illustrations equating the hours of the Virgin (for which there is text) and the hours of the Passion (no text). There are illustrations for the hours of Saint Louis, beloved of royal ladies of the time. And finally, in every margin there are gay drolleries. All are superbly and delicately drawn and painted in grisaille with touches of color.

This manuscript is a landmark in the history of French painting not only because of its superb quality but because it fused into a new style all the currents of its time. The compositions in Italian painting, especially Duccio's, the most advanced conception of interior space, the humorous, whimsical marginal illuminations so popular in England and north France, all are here integrated into the Paris tradition of elegance and good taste.

Jeanne d'Évreux willed the book to King Charles V of France, who in turn gave it to his brother Jean, duke of Berry. More recently it was owned by Baron Maurice de Rothschild.

An inscription on the first page of the *Belles Heures* manuscript (see fig. 77) states: "These Hours were made to the order of the very excellent and mighty Prince Jehan, son of the king of France, duke of Berry." It is listed in the Duke of Berry's inventory, which was begun in 1413, as "a *belles heures*, very well and richly illustrated." Several pages of the manuscript also bear the duke's coat of arms and his emblems, the bear and the swan; his motto *Le temps venra* is included on the calendar page for December.

There are 224 folios in the book with 94 full-page and 54 column illustrations, as well as the calendar vignettes and border illumina-

tions: a whole gallery of medieval paintings, almost as fresh as
when they were first painted by Pol de Limbourg and his brothers
about 1410–1413. The attribution to these illustrators is made on
the basis of the similarity of the illustrations to the famous *Très
Riches Heures* in Chantilly which an inventory of 1416 states was
made by "Pol and his brothers."

77. *The Belles Heures of the Duke of Berry, illuminated by the
Limbourg brothers. Franco-Netherlandish, about 1410–1413*

The Limbourgs were born in Gelder in the duchy of Limbourg
(now Belgium); they worked in Paris and at the court of Philip of
Burgundy before joining the entourage of the Duke of Berry.
They were among the favorite *enlumineurs* of the duke, as his account books and inventories testify. They were brilliant colorists,
dramatic and inventive storytellers, experimenters in the painting
of atmospheric depth. Although many of the pages of the *Belles
Heures* show strong Italian influence, they remain essentially northern in spirit and in style. The manuscript ranks among the master-
pieces of the Middle Ages.

After the death of Jean, duke of Berry, the book was purchased by Yolande of Aragon, queen of Sicily and duchess of Anjou. In the nineteenth century it was in the possession of the Ailly family from whom Baron Edmond de Rothschild bought it in 1880. It was acquired for The Cloisters from Baron Maurice de Rothschild in 1954.

The pages of both manuscripts are turned every few weeks. This is essential to the well-being of the books and affords visitors an opportunity to see, over a period of time, all the important illustrations in the manuscripts.

IVORIES. Ivory statuettes, diptychs, and shrines were often used to furnish small private chapels in churches and homes. Diptychs could also be easily folded and taken on a journey. The ivories shown in the Treasury of The Cloisters, all of the fourteenth century, have been borrowed from the rich collection of medieval ivories at the main building of the Metropolitan Museum.

Second Room

EMBROIDERED ROUNDELS. These embroideries, all of silk and metal threads on linen, represent a high point in the art of "needle painting" as it was practiced in the Middle Ages. With many companion pieces, they probably once enriched a liturgical vestment, altar frontal or dorsal. In the seventeenth century they were cut out and reused on other vestments. Two of the roundels represent scenes from the legend of Saint Catherine. In one she is shown a picture of the Virgin and Child and is baptized by a hermit monk. In the other the Empress and Prince Porphyry go to visit Catherine, who has been thrown into prison by the emperor. These embroideries are close in style to the early works of Rogier van der Weyden and can be dated about 1430-1440.

The other two roundels represent scenes in the legend of Saint Martin. In one Saint Martin explains his faith to brigands who are about to put him to death. In the other he exhorts the empress, who is kneeling at his feet. These embroideries are different in style and workmanship from the Saint Catherine series. There is a French influence mixed with the Flemish here, but the date is about the same, 1430–1440.

THE MITER. Until the early 1930s this miter was in the treasury of the Benedictine abbey of Saint Peter in Salzburg. Although the miter was the liturgical head covering for bishops, certain abbots had permission to wear it also; the privilege was conferred on the abbot of Saint Peter of Salzburg in 1231. In 1266 a papal decree forbade abbots to wear miters with jewels. Hence this miter was probably made between 1231 and 1266. It is fashioned of white Persian silk with silk and silver-gilt bands and lappets of a weave usually associated with Sicily in the twelfth century; the ornaments of silver-gilt are jeweled with corals. On the borders is woven a hymn to the Virgin, which reads in part: "O guiding Star of the Sea, rightly invoked by those who have lost their way, enlighten my heart that I may know the divine will. Inspire me with ardor which nourishes the highest love.... Drive away from me the mighty fiends, O Blessed Virgin ... thou who, higher than the heavens, art singing praises to the Lord."

THE BONE BOX. The reliquary box mounted on a wooden core was also for many years in the treasury of the abbey of Saint Peter in Salzburg. Its shape probably derives from the purses or bags made of precious textiles in which relics were kept and carried from place to place. Originally the openwork patterns of the bone plaques were silhouetted against gilded copper foil, some of which remains. Traces of blue and vermilion paint can still be seen accenting the borders of the designs. The flat, geometric style is similar to

ivory carvings and architectural sculptures of northern Italy. The box has been dated as early as the tenth century; it is certainly no later than the eleventh.

THE PAIR OF ANGELS (fig. 78), of the thirteenth century, recall the famous smiling angels of the cathedral of Reims.Although they are only twenty-nine inches high, they possess the monumentality of thirteenth century cathedral statues, and at the same time they are fashioned with the delicacy and elegance of fine ivory carvings. The bold, deeply cut drapery folds, which sweep and fall in a variety of forms and patterns, give dignity to the graceful long-limbed figures with their small heads, curling hair, and delicate, idealized features. These two oak angels are among the master-pieces of the late thirteenth century school of Reims. At one time they had wings, they were painted in gold and rich colors, and they probably held in their hands candlesticks or instruments of the Passion. They are undoubtedly companion pieces to the angel in the Louvre, an oak statue of about the same size.

78. Angels. French (School of Reims), late XIII *century*

THE BOPPARD ROOM

THE six stained glass panels from the church of the Carmelite convent of Saint Severinus at Boppard, on the Rhine, form the most brilliant ensemble of late Gothic stained glass in this country. While this is not the finest glass the Middle Ages produced, the fact that it has been possible to obtain, almost intact, large panels of such outstanding quality is remarkable. Comparatively little of this fragile material has survived.

The six saints portrayed in these panels (see fig. 79) stand in elaborate canopied niches. They are, from left to right: a bishop saint with a key and a crosier, trampling on a dragon symbolic of evil; the Virgin, with ears of wheat on her robe and at her side an angel with a crown of flowers and a prisoner in a tower; another bishop saint; Saint Catherine of Alexandria with the attributes of her martyrdom, a wheel and a sword; Saint Dorothea of Caesarea, holding a basket of red flowers from the celestial garden, and at her side the infant Christ; and Saint Barbara carrying her attribute, a tower. In the lower sections there are the archangel Michael trampling a dragon and weighing souls; a silver shield with a red key; a pilgrim saint and Saint James the Greater, and in the lower corners heraldic shields bearing emblems (*Hausmarken*); the arms of a guild of coopers—a red shield with a golden compass, two silver mallets, and a golden barrel hung beneath—held by two angels; a representation of the Holy Trinity; and two angels supporting a red shield with a silver star. The colors predominating in the windows are red, blue, golden yellow, and shaded white. The white turreted canopies are silhouetted against red or blue sky colors, which also appear in the side panels of the niches and contrast strongly with the white mantles the saints wear; spots of green and

156

79. Stained glass from Boppard. Rhenish, 1425–1450

purple are scattered throughout, especially in the costume accessories and the narrow borders.

The panels appear to have been made for the polygonal choir of the church of Saint Severinus, which was the second oldest Carmelite house in Germany, founded before 1270. On the basis of style and various dates in the history of the church they may be assigned to the second quarter of the fifteenth century. After the secularization of Church property in the Rhineland in the Napoleonic era, the glass was sold. Not being fashionable, it was packed away until 1871. In 1875 it was acquired and restored by Frédéric Spitzer of Paris. At the famous sale of the Spitzer collection in 1893 it was again sold; after that, except for a brief period of exhibition at the Musée des Arts Décoratifs, in Paris, it was not on public view until it was installed at The Cloisters.

The painted section of the pine ceiling in the Boppard Room comes from the Tyrol and is of the late fifteenth or early sixteenth century. The monogram of Christ, IHS, in the central panel suggests that the ceiling was originally used in an ecclesiastical, not a secular, building, although such ceilings are more usual in domestic interiors.

THE SPANISH ALABASTER RETABLE (see figs. 80, 81) is appropriately shown with the stained glass from Boppard, for Rhenish artists were active in Spain in the fifteenth century. This retable, purchased in Paris by J. Pierpont Morgan, who presented it to the Museum in 1909, comes from the Archbishop's Palace in Saragossa. The variegated alabaster of which it is made has acquired a yellow tone. Such alabaster is frequently seen in sculpture from northern Spain, where it was quarried extensively along the Ebro River.

Traces of paint indicate that the canopied gables were originally rich with polychromy. The scenes below represent Saint Martin dividing his cloak with a beggar; Christ appearing to Saint Martin;

80. Christ appearing to Saint Martin.
    Detail from alabaster retable. Spanish, xv century

81. Detail from alabaster retable

the day of Pentecost, when the Holy Spirit descended upon the
apostles in tongues of fire; the miraculous escape of Saint Thecla,
a convert of Saint Paul, from death at the stake; and Saint Thecla
listening to Saint Paul preaching. A painting may once have surmounted the stonework. The panel with the instruments of the
Passion and the two figures holding heraldic shields bearing the
arms of Don Dalmacio de Mur, who became archbishop of Saragossa in 1434, have been incorporated in an altar constructed in
accordance with a photograph of the original altar in the Archbishop's Palace. The retable is well known in the literature of
Spanish sculpture.

THE BURG WEILER ALTARPIECE hanging above the retable is the work of an anonymous artist of the middle Rhenish school active in the third quarter of the fifteenth century. It was painted about 1470 for the chapel of a castle called Burg Weiler, which commands a tributary of the Neckar a few miles above Heilbronn. The altarpiece remained in the castle until 1934.

On either side of the Virgin and Child in the central panel are: Saint Apollonia with her attributes, the pincers and an extracted tooth; Saint Barbara with chalice and Host; Saint Catherine with sword and broken wheel; and Saint Lawrence with the gridiron, instrument of his martyrdom. On the left wing are the less familiar pilgrim saints, Jodokus and Wendelinus, who were patrons of pilgrims and protectors of cattle. On the right wing are Saint Sebastian with bow and arrows, and the soldier Saint Maurice, leader of the Theban legion that was wiped out by the Romans when the soldiers refused to observe certain pagan rites. The scene of their martyrdom is painted on the reverse of the left wing; on the reverse of the right wing is the figure of a bishop, Saint Theodulus, who built the abbey of Saint Maurice on the site of the martyrdom of the legion.

The altarpiece is in unusually intact and fresh condition, its brilliant colors unfaded through the years.

THE LIMESTONE DOORWAY leading to the Hall of the Unicorn Tapestries is decorated in the style called flamboyant Gothic. Its strong pointed arch, composed of large stones laid in eleven courses and held in place by a keystone, is gracefully carved with bases and columnlike moldings that emphasize the outline of the opening. The superstructure is ornamented with cusps and pinnacles that enhance the feeling of verticality. The two parallel cornices at the top provide a transition to the wall above. Although this upper part of the doorway has the appearance of a lintel, it is the arch itself that carries the load of the wall.

THE HALL OF THE UNICORN TAPESTRIES

THE Hunt of the Unicorn, a series of six tapestries and fragments of another, is among the most prized of our inheritances from the Middle Ages. In design, in beauty of coloring, and in intensity of pictorial realism these hangings form the most superb ensemble of late medieval tapestries in existence.

Five of them were in all probability made for Anne of Brittany (1476–1514) in celebration of her marriage to Louis XII (1462–1515) on January 8, 1499, whereby Anne, widow of Charles VIII, became queen of France for the second time. The two tapestries on the window wall—somewhat later in date and representing the first and seventh scenes in the series—may have been added to the original set when Francis I (1494–1547) married Anne's daughter and heir in 1514.

Many allusions to the courtship and marriage of Anne and Louis may be found incorporated in the Hunt of the Unicorn. Prominent in the design is Anne's cipher, the letters *A* and *E* (with the *E* reversed), the first and last letters of Anne's name and also of her motto, *A ma vie*. These letters, tied with a cordelière, a twisted cord or rope, appear on the average five times in each of the six complete tapestries and once in the fragments. The same letters without the cordelière appear on one of the dog collars, and the letter *A* alone appears on two dog collars. The cordelière was worn by Saint Francis of Assisi, and Franciscan monks were called Cordeliers. Francis, duke of Brittany, Anne's grandfather, used this emblem in evidence of his devotion to his patron saint. Anne also used it in every possible way; it appears with her arms, with the letter *A* in decorations, and as part of her dress. In 1498 she founded the chivalric order of the Dames de la Cordelière, which she bestowed upon the principal ladies of her court. Louis's colors, red and white (silver), are used in the cordelières in the five tapestries made for Anne.

The unicorn, the fabulous and picturesque animal depicted in these tapestries, appears in the ancient folklore of India and the Near East. Ctesias, a Greek physician of the early fourth century B.C., described it, for the first time in literature, as an animal "exceedingly swift and powerful" which "no creature, neither the

82. Second tapestry. The unicorn at the fountain.
  Franco-Flemish, late XV century

83. Huntsman. Detail from the third tapestry. The unicorn tries to escape

horse nor any other" could overtake. The elder Pliny described it as an "exceedingly wild beast," with one black horn two cubits long projecting from the middle of its forehead, which, by reputation, could not be "taken alive." In the Middle Ages it was believed that the unicorn could be caught only by a virgin. It was related that this wild and unconquerable animal became tame when confronted by a maiden; it would lay its head in her lap and was thus easily taken by the hunter. The story is told in various versions of the *Physiologus*, a zoological and botanical encyclopedia popular in Europe from the fifth century on, and in the bestiaries based upon it. In these accounts the unicorn is a symbol of Christ, the virgin is the Virgin Mary, the huntsman is the angel Gabriel, and the story of the hunt is an allegory of the Incarnation. Beginning with Richard de Fournival's *Bestiaire d'amour* in the thirteenth century, there was an increasing tendency to interpret the legend of the unicorn caught by a maiden as an allegory of courtly love. In view of the fact that the Unicorn tapestries are thought to have been woven as a wedding gift, it is reasonable to suppose that at least one of the themes running through the elaborate portrayal of the hunt is that of courtship and marriage.

The first tapestry shows the party of hunters, with varlets holding the dogs in leash, setting forth in search of the unicorn. A small figure in the upper right-hand corner is beckoning to his followers, probably to tell them that the unicorn has been sighted. The principal figure (the second from the left) is a young man of about twenty, probably Francis I, wearing the royal colors of France: red, white, and blue. He is accompanied by two companions carrying spears and wearing his colors: red, tan (yellow), and blue. The millefleurs background, a flowery mead on the edge of a forest, is elaborated with a variety of plants typical of late fifteenth or early sixteenth century tapestries; these are drawn with a freedom and grace entirely lacking in the rigid, comparatively expressionless figures. In this and the other tapestries in the series there are over a hundred

84. Hunting dog. Detail from the fourth tapestry.
The unicorn defends himself

distinct kinds of plants, about eighty-five of which are identifiable. They recall Anne's particular interest in flowers. Charles VIII planted gardens for her at Amboise, and Louis XII built other gardens for her at Blois.

In the second tapestry (fig. 82) the hunters have surrounded the unicorn, which kneels and dips its horn in a stream flowing from a fountain, a symbol of the waters of eternal life. This scene is described in the Greek bestiaries and is based on the old belief that the unicorn's horn would absorb poison. John of Hesse, who went

85. Heron. Detail from the fourth tapestry.
  The unicorn defends himself

to Jerusalem in 1389, records: "And even in our times it is said, venomous animals poison the water after the setting of the sun, so that the good animals cannot drink of it, but in the morning after the sunrise, comes the unicorn and dips his horn into the stream driving away the poison from it. . . . This I have seen for myself." The animals included in the tapestry are a lion and a lioness, a panther, a civet, a hyena, a stag, and two rabbits. These animals are themselves symbolic; for example, the lion stands for the strength of Christ, the panther for his sweet savor, and the stag, destroyer of snakes, for his power over evil. Perched on the rim of the fountain are two pheasants, a European goldfinch, and a swallow. In this and the succeeding four tapestries, the human figures are treated in a more adroit and realistic manner than in the first, indicating that the latter was not part of the original series.

In the third tapestry (see fig. 83) the unicorn tries to escape but is surrounded by spearmen who approach from all sides. Anne's flag, which bears a black cross on a white (silver) field, flies from a gable of the castle in the background. The dog collars with *A* and *E* and one with Louis's three silver-gilt fleurs-de-lis, the royal insignia, on a red band identify the dogs' owners. The monogram ЃⱤ noticeably different from the others actually woven in the tapestries, may be the initials of François de la Rochefoucauld or Francis I (Franciscus Rex). The only surviving fragment of the original border is to be found at the lower left-hand corner of this tapestry.

In the fourth tapestry (see figs. 84–85) the unicorn, at bay, gores a greyhound with its horn. Anne is heralded in the inscription AVE REGINA C[OELORUM], the salutation to the Virgin, the Queen of Heaven, on the scabbard of the hunter at the extreme left (see fig. 84). On the collar of the dog at the right of this huntsman is a corresponding salutation to Louis, O F[R]ANC[ORUM] RE[X].

In the fifth tapestry (fig. 86), of which only fragments remain, the hand of the virgin is shown fondling the neck of the unicorn, while a half-concealed huntsman signals with his horn to the other pursuers. The sleeve of the maiden is made of the same brocade as the dress worn by Anne in the sixth tapestry. The figure behind the unicorn is one of Anne's attendants. The introduction of Anne in this scene as the maiden who makes possible the capture of the wild beast also associates her with the Virgin in the Christian allegory of the Incarnation. The monogram of Christ, IHS, on one of the dog collars bears witness to the designer's intention of using the unicorn as a symbol of Christ in this story.

86. Fragments of the fifth tapestry. The unicorn is captured by the maiden

In the sixth tapestry (see fig. 87) the unicorn is slain and brought to Anne and Louis, portrayed life-size, standing arm in arm in front of the castle. Though these are not portraits according to present-day conceptions, they bear striking resemblances to other contemporary representations of Anne and Louis. Anne and her ladies in waiting wear the characteristic Breton headdress of the period. Unlike other queens of France, who wore white for mourning, Anne, as in this tapestry, wore a black undercap. The gold chain with a pendent cross around her neck, the yellow-brown, red, and gold brocade of her dress, the brown fur, probably sable, lining her wide sleeves, the blue girdle, and the rosary attached thereto are familiar attributes of Anne as she is shown in other pictures. These items are also noted in extant inventories and expense accounts. The squirrel which is so prominent in the lower left-hand corner of the tapestry is actually held by Anne in other representations and may have some special significance that is not as yet apparent.

The colors of Louis's costume are particularly striking. The king wears a white hat, a short red robe or dress, and red and white striped stockings. After his marriage to Anne, Louis added her color, white, to his own, which had been red and yellow, and often used red and white exclusively. Among the several flags flying from the castle buildings the one to the left, above the figure of the queen, again shows a black cross, this time on a yellow and gold ground. From the next roof flies Louis's flag with a rather haphazardly drawn red porcupine on a field of white (silver). At the far right are two pennants bearing Louis's colors.

The seventh tapestry (fig. 88) can be interpreted as a symbol of the risen Christ. It shows the unicorn alone, alive but with his wounds apparent, within an enclosure probably signifying the *hortus conclusus*, a symbol of the Blessed Virgin and the Incarnation. Since the unicorn is leashed with a golden chain, symbol of marriage, to a tree bearing pomegranates, symbols of fertility, this tapestry is also to be interpreted as the consummation of marriage.

87. *The unicorn is brought to Louis* XII *of France and Anne of Brittany.*
Detail of the sixth tapestry

It is stylistically similar to the first and is also contemporary with it.

The tapestries are in an excellent state of preservation. The original weaving, except here and there, and then only in comparatively small, restricted areas, is almost as fresh as it was the day the tapestries left the looms. There are occasional restorations of unknown date; other than those made under the Museum's supervision, they seem to be eighteenth or nineteenth century work. To judge from the small fragment of original border in the third tapestry, all of them were framed as they are at present, with two narrow bands of white and red and an outer band of shaded blue, the traditional color of royal France.

The subject matter is more appealing and the execution more vigorous than in most other works of art of the period. The scenes are treated pictorially, in each case fulfilling the requirements of the composition without too consistent an emphasis on perspective; but the individual figures, flowers, birds, and animals are naturalistically rendered. The velvets and brocades of the costumes, the costume accessories, the dog collars, and other details are executed with many refinements of technique. The profusion of details and the harmonious colors are masterfully arranged. The distribution of the reds, yellows, blues, and orange, together with the emphasis on the white unicorn, is as dramatic as it is pleasant; and the green and blue-green foliage is deftly worked into the background. The painstakingly prepared vegetable dyes allowed a range in color rarely surpassed in the most elaborate contemporary paintings and manuscript illuminations. Silver and silver-gilt threads are but sparingly employed, and then only to enrich certain details. The closely woven wool and silk threads, varying from about sixteen to nineteen ribs to the inch, produce an effect obtainable in no other medium.

It is as extraordinary as it is regrettable that it has not yet been possible to discover precisely by whom and where these tapestries were made. With works of such excellence it may also seem in-

88. Seventh tapestry. The unicorn in captivity. French, early XVI *century*

credible that the artists who designed them should not have been identified. There have been many attempts to establish a French or a Flemish origin for these tapestries, but no sufficient evidence has been forthcoming. That the Unicorn tapestries at The Cloisters bear strong resemblances to such hangings as the millefleurs tapestries depicting concert scenes in the Gobelins museum, the Louvre, and the museum of Angers is certain. They also recall such hunting tapestries as those of the Duke of Devonshire, now at the Victoria and Albert Museum, and the Lady with the Unicorn series in the Cluny museum in Paris. All these tapestries have definitely Flemish characteristics, and at such centers as Tournai in the fifteenth century there was unprecedented activity. While the Cluny tapestries, generally ascribed to the Loire Valley, are closer than any others to the first and seventh of the Cloisters series, none of the comparable tapestries are like the five made for Anne.

All seven tapestries, possibly presented by Francis to his godfather François de la Rochefoucauld, belonged to the Rochefoucauld family for generations. They are first mentioned in an inventory of 1728, which states that they were at that time in the château of Verteuil, one of the ancestral seats of the Rochefoucauld family. (The same inventory indicates that they were in need of repairs.) Five of the tapestries hung in the great room of the new wing, and two others were in the great lower hall near the chapel. During the French Revolution they were taken from the castle and, according to one account, used for a time to protect potatoes from freezing. Portions now missing from the original fabric of the tapestries were probably cut away in 1793 when the Société Populaire of Ruffec sent to the Société Populaire of Verteuil an edict ordering that all the paintings at Verteuil and all the tapestries having royal insignia be destroyed. In the nineteenth century the tapestries were once again acquired by the Rochefoucaulds. They remained at Verteuil until the early 1920s, when they were purchased by John D. Rockefeller, Jr., who cherished them in his New

York residence until he presented them to the Museum for The Cloisters.

THE STAINED GLASS. Little evidence of the use of heraldry survives in the Unicorn tapestries; its fullest development, however, is represented in an unusual set of stained glass panels. Four of them contain the armorial achievements of the Emperor Maximilian; of his son Philip the Fair, king of Castile; of his grandson, the young Prince Charles, later the Emperor Charles V; and of one of his councilors, Henry, count of Nassau. Another panel, not exhibited, shows the arms of Maximilian's chamberlain, Roland Le Febure, lord of Tamise and viscount of Haerlebeque. All five were living during Philip's reign (1504–1506) and the panels were probably painted at that time. It has been said that the glass comes from one of the castles in Ghent.

In these panels the delicate, transparent colors are combined with the strong outlines of the leading in an unusually harmonious arrangement. They also show a most accomplished use of several techniques: flashing with various yellow stains; cutwork, in which the glass is rubbed with hard stone; and the insertion of glass within glass by adroit leading. Except in the more complicated shields the heraldic details are stained or both stained and painted in black, yellow, white, and red on single panes of white glass. Such glass depends for effect more upon painting than upon the juxtaposition of small pieces of molded glass in various colors, the technique used in earlier periods.

THE MANTELPIECE AND WINDOW. A monumental fifteenth century mantelpiece from Alençon is installed in the south wall of this room. Opposite is a window from a late Gothic house in Cluny. In addition to the leaded glass in this window, described above, there are sheets of modern glass specially made to filter out the deleterious rays of the sun.

THE BURGOS TAPESTRY HALL

THE BURGOS TAPESTRY of the Nativity (see fig. 89), one of a series representing the Salvation of Man, comes from the cathedral of Burgos in Spain. The set is believed to have consisted of eight tapestries and to have been reproduced several times from the same cartoons. The Cloisters tapestry is the only known one of the series that represents the Nativity and related subjects. Also from Burgos cathedral and now in the main building of the Metropolitan Museum is another tapestry of this series, the Redemption of Man, illustrating allegories of the conflict of vices and virtues.

The scenes in the Nativity tapestry are arranged in two registers. In the upper one, at the far left, is God the Father, wearing a crown and holding a scepter, with figures of Humility and Charity; at the right Peace and Justice are embracing. Next is God the Father enthroned and surrounded by figures, including Truth and Humility, who hold a mirror in which the Virgin is seen kneeling in adoration before the young Christ child. At the right the angel of the Annunciation holds a banderole inscribed with the salutation to the Virgin. Other virtues and angels are included in the group. In the third scene of this register Joseph, accompanied by Mary, presents the Roman tax collector with "a penny in acknowledgment that he was subject to the empire of Rome," as recorded in *The Golden Legend*. In the fourth scene the Virgin is surrounded by the three figures of the Trinity; at the left the angel of the Annunciation kneels before Humility. At the far right are three astrologers of the East studying the prophecies of Balaam, and beyond them the three Magi beneath the star in which they see the Child.

In the first scene of the second register Man, in fetters, is shown with Nature, Misery, Hope, Abraham, Isaac, and Jacob. In the background is Temptation, holding a spear in one hand and a key in the other. The central group depicts the marriage of the Virgin Mary and Joseph. In the foreground of the third scene is the Christ child and behind the kneeling Virgin are the figures of Humility and Chastity. In the extreme lower corners of the tapestry are the prophets Micah (?) and Isaiah holding banderoles with inscrip-

*89. The Nativity. Detail of tapestry from Burgos cathedral.
Flemish (Brussels), about 1495*

tions which may be read: *Dominus egredietur de loco sancto suo.*
Isaias XXVI (The Lord cometh forth out of his holy place. Isaiah 26)
and *Parvulus natus est nobis. Isaias IX* (Unto us a child is born. Isaiah
9). As the words of the first inscription, except *sancto*, are identical
in Isaiah 26:21 and Micah 1:3, the text was probably intended to be
a quotation from Micah rather than Isaiah and an identification of
the figure as that prophet.

According to tradition, these magnificent tapestries were woven
in Brussels about 1495 for the Emperor Maximilian, who presented
them to his son Philip the Fair, to commemorate his marriage with
Joanna, the daughter of Ferdinand and Isabella, in 1496. The double
eagle of the Holy Roman Empire, woven in a prominent place,
lends credence to this story. Furthermore, it is recorded that Pieter
van Aelst, the famous tapestry weaver and dealer of Brussels, went
to Spain with Philip on his first visit in 1502 and that, after the death
of Philip at Burgos in 1506, Van Aelst was imprisoned by Ferdinand
for taking some of Philip's tapestries and putting them in what he
called a safe place. It is known that the streets of Burgos were hung
with tapestries when Philip and Joanna came there in 1506 and that
Van Aelst, with four assistants, was in charge of decorating the
abodes of the royal couple, but it has not yet been possible to deter-
mine how and when the Nativity tapestry and three others of the
series came into the possession of Burgos cathedral. The similarity
of these tapestries to other productions of the Van Aelst workshops
suggests their attribution to this great weaver, who is celebrated for
having been entrusted with the making of tapestries from cartoons
by Raphael some years after the death of Philip.

THE CHARLES VIII TAPESTRY. This tapestry is called
the Glorification of King Charles VIII because it has been decided
that the principal figure, appearing at least five times, represents the
French monarch in his youth (see fig. 90). It was a custom of French
kings in the Middle Ages to identify themselves with distant fore-

90. Detail from tapestry of the Glorification of King Charles VIII.
Flemish (Brussels), about 1490

bears and to have themselves represented in the guise of Old Testament and historical personages. The custom adds to both the complexity and the interest of the scenes portrayed in this tapestry.

In 1483, when he was thirteen, Charles succeeded his father, Louis XI, as king of France; his sister, Anne de Beaujeu, was appointed regent. At twelve Charles had been married to three-year-old Margaret of Austria, daughter of Maximilian and granddaughter of Frederic III. In secular terms these are the dramatis personae of the tapestry. Charles appears five times (perhaps a sixth as King Arthur); he can always be identified by his crown, but his features vary considerably. In the second scene from the left, Anne de Beaujeu is depicted ascending the steps of her brother's throne. In the large central scene Maximilian and Frederic III are in the group facing the dignitaries of the Church. Margaret appears at the right of the scene, wearing a pendant with the double-headed eagle of the Holy Roman Empire; she seems here to be about ten years old. In 1491 Charles renounced his marriage to Margaret and married Anne of Brittany, who appears in the Unicorn tapestries at The Cloisters; for this reason the Charles VIII tapestry is dated before 1491.

The inscription REOON (with letters backward), boldly woven on the leg of the page in the left corner of the tapestry, is probably the signature of the designer, Jan van Roome. The head and shoulders of the man standing just behind Maximilian may be his self-portrait.

The iconographic scheme is a complicated one, based in part on the popular fourteenth century *Speculum humanae salvationis* (Mirror of Man's Salvation), which explains the fall and redemption of man by parallels taken mainly from the Old Testament. At the marriage of Charles to Margaret of Austria a sermon preached by the abbot of Saint-Bertin compared the union to that of King Ahasuerus with Esther. The three scenes at the left of the tapestry represent incidents from the story of Esther and Ahasuerus, who, according to the *Speculum*, were prototypes of the Virgin Mary and Christ. Above, Mordecai petitions the king to rescind the order for the death of the Jews, and Esther and Ahasuerus watch while the new decree is written. Below, the chamberlains who plotted against Ahasuerus are arrested in the presence of the king and queen. The next scene, extending the full height of the tapestry, may represent Esther and Ahasuerus with Haman standing in the foreground.

The next scene to the right represents the Emperor Augustus (Octavian) being shown the vision of the Virgin holding in her arms the Christ child who would rule the world and redeem mankind. The three compartments above should be considered together with the three corresponding ones on the opposite side of the central panel of the tapestry. There are the three Christian heroes, Charlemagne alone on the left, and Godfrey of Bouillon and Arthur together on the right. There are also two parables of the kingdom of heaven from the Gospel of Saint Matthew: at the left is a man digging for "a treasure hid in a field"; on the right is the "householder who bringeth forth out of his treasure things new and old." And finally, there are Adam and Eve, whose sin brought about the Fall and made necessary the coming of a Redeemer. In the central section the Redeemer sits enthroned in paradise with Mercy carrying a lily and Justice a sword, while a company of clergy and laity adore him.

To the right, the story of Esther and Ahasuerus is continued: Esther intercedes for the lives of her people, and Haman plots against the Jews, while above, the king of Moab sacrifices his eldest son to save his people. This incident, according to the *Speculum*, prefigured the Crucifixion.

The large scene at the extreme right was formerly interpreted as one from the life of Charlemagne. More probably it represents the Emperor Augustus enthroned; the imperial eagle above his head carries the dove of peace in its claws. In one of the scenes

above, the emperor directs work on the Ara Coeli, which he is said
to have ordered constructed after seeing the vision of the Christ
child. The scene may also refer to Tubalcain, who was believed to
have first "made sculptures and gravings in metal." Tubalcain's
sister Noema was supposed to have founded the craft of textile
making; it may be she who is shown here with her ladies and their
baskets of wool. According to the *Speculum*, Tubalcain and
Noema foretold the joys of paradise, where their skill in art would
be among the delights of the blessed.

There are several tapestries that repeat with variations the central
portions of the Charles VIII tapestry. One is in the cathedral of La
Seo in Saragossa, another in the Cinquantenaire museum in Brussels, and a third, known as the Mazarin tapestry, in the National
Gallery in Washington.

The Charles VIII tapestry is believed to be the longest medieval
wool, silk, and metal thread tapestry in existence. Sometime before the second half of the nineteenth century it was cut and made
into three separate panels. The right section, which hung for many
years in the dining room of George Blumenthal's house at Park
Avenue and 70th Street in New York and came to the Museum
with his other munificent gifts, was long known as the "Charlemagne" tapestry. This piece and the central section have been traced
to the château of Bazoches-du-Morvan (Nièvre), whence they were
sold soon after 1900 by the Marquis Henri de Vibraye. His grandson has been unable to discover any provenance going back to an
earlier generation. The central section came from Bazoches,
through the Engel-Gros collection, Château de Ripaille, on the
Lake of Geneva, and an auction at the Georges Petit Gallery in
1921, to the Walters Art Gallery in Baltimore. The left section,
long unrecognized on the New York art market as belonging with
the other two, was formerly in the possession of Baron Arthur
Schickler, who about 1872 had placed it in his castle at Martinvast,
near Cherbourg.

THE ARMORIAL TAPESTRY bears the arms of John, Lord Dynham (1433-1501), who lived during the Wars of the Roses and held high office under five English kings without losing either his lands or his head. He was appointed treasurer of the realm in 1486 by Henry VII and in 1487 was made Knight of the Order of the Garter.

In heraldic terms the arms are described as gules (red), four fusils (lozenges) ermine, the whole surrounded by the Garter bearing the motto *Hony soit qui male y pense*. The large central shield is supported by two stags. The crest is an ermine standing between two lighted candles on an ermine-lined cap of estate. The mantling is also of ermine. In the upper right shield the Dynham arms impale the Arches arms, gules, three arches argent (silver), two conjoined. Lord Dynham's mother was the daughter of Sir Richard Arches. Lord Dynham's badge, the broken-off topcastle of a medieval warship armed with five spears or arrows and flying the cross of Saint George, is repeated several times; it recalls his many exploits at sea.

The tapestry is probably of Tournai workmanship and dates between 1487, when Lord Dynham was made Knight of the Garter, and 1501, when he died.

THE EWERS. The two large silver-gilt ewers (see fig. 92), standing upon a credenza that fills the space where part of the Charles VIII tapestry is missing, were made for Hartmann von Stockheim, German Master of the Order of Teutonic Knights from 1499 to 1510. According to early inventories, the Hartmann coat of arms formerly appeared on the shields held by the "wild men." For centuries the ewers were preserved in the treasury of the Teutonic Knights; shortly before World War II they were sold in Vienna to a private collector. Of Rhenish workmanship, about 1500, they are unique for size and quality among vessels of this sort. They were probably ordered to commemorate a special occasion, were used perhaps once, and then retired to the treasury of the order. Animals with dragon heads form the handles and enameled "wild men" with clubs and shields rise from the battlements on the lids.

THE RELIQUARY BUST of a female saint (fig. 91), with most of its original painting and gilding intact, was one of several similar reliquary heads undoubtedly carved for a large composite altarpiece. Such altarpieces had niches in each of which a reliquary bust was placed; the relic could be seen through a glass- or crystal-covered opening in the front. This bust, with its mannered elegance and intricate detail, was probably produced in a Flemish workshop for export to Spain. It is strikingly similar in costume and style to several Brabantine sculptures of the early sixteenth century, particularly a Saint Barbara of about 1510 in the church of Notre-Dame-aux-Riches-Claires in Brussels.

91. *Reliquary bust. Flemish (Brabant), early* XVI *century*

92. *Ewer. Rhenish, about 1500*

THE SPANISH ROOM

This room, called the Spanish Room (fig. 93) because of the painted Spanish ceiling, has been furnished as a domestic interior such as one sees in late medieval paintings. Many of the objects here are similar to those shown in the Campin altarpiece, the most important work of art in the room and one of the greatest treasures at The Cloisters.

Authentic Gothic domestic ceilings are rare. The painted one here, dating from the fifteenth century, came from a small *palacio* at Illescas, the halfway stopping place between Madrid and Toledo. It is said to have come from a bedroom occupied by Francis I of France when he was a prisoner of the Emperor Charles V. It is related to the late fourteenth century ceiling covering the cloister walk of the monastery of Santo Domingo de Silos, though the latter is simpler in construction. Both ceilings have beams and paneling similarly arranged. Both are of red pine coated with a thin gesso foundation and painted; the lower frieze of the Cloisters ceiling was later repainted with animal motifs much like those of the beams and frieze at Silos.

The bronze chandelier hanging from the ceiling must have been used to light the home of a wealthy family—for candles were a luxury in the Middle Ages. It was cast in separate pieces; each arm has assembly marks corresponding with marks on the central shaft. The entire surface was hand-tooled and the rough parts made smooth before the final polishing. It is probably of Flemish workmanship. A similar fifteenth century chandelier is shown in the portrait of Jan Arnolfini and his wife painted by Jan van Eyck in 1434.

The laver with double spout and ringed handle for hanging in a niche is similar to the one shown in the Campin altarpiece; such vessels were used for washing the hands. This one is probably Flemish.

The candlesticks are similar to the one shown in the Virgin's room in the Campin altarpiece. They may be German or Flemish. All the bronzes are polished as they would have been in the Middle Ages and as they appear in the paintings.

The high-backed bench of walnut and oak is unusually well preserved. The finials consist of two dogs and two lions like those on the bench in the Annunciation scene of the painting. Lions in the Middle Ages were symbolic of courage, dogs of fidelity.

The iron birdcage of the fifteenth century is the only one known to have survived the Middle Ages.

THE ALTARPIECE BY ROBERT CAMPIN (fig. 94) has long been world-famous, an acknowledged early Flemish masterpiece. Purchased in Bruges in 1820 by the Prince of Arenberg, it was later inherited by the Merode family who held it for two generations. Until it was acquired for The Cloisters it had been inaccessible to art lovers and art historians for decades, though illustrated and discussed in countless publications.

The central scene of this small triptych is the Annunciation; at the right is Saint Joseph in his workshop (see fig. 95), and at the left are two donors kneeling in adoration.

Campin is regarded as the initiator of the trend of realism in Flemish panel painting. In this altarpiece every object, no matter how humble, has been painted meticulously so that its essential character and its own particular beauty of form and texture is brought out. The sense of reality is enhanced by the cast shadows and the reflections of light on the surfaces. Fascinated as he was by details, however, Campin subordinated them all to this remarkable composition in space and pattern and color and light. He rejoiced in painting the material world and was the first to place the

93. The Spanish Room

94. The Annunciation altarpiece by Robert Campin. Flemish, about 1425

Annunciation in a contemporary bourgeois living room, but he included in that room many objects of symbolic significance. For instance, the laver is a symbol of Mary's purity, like the bouquet of lilies. The candle is a symbol of Christ, and the candlestick represents the Virgin Mary who bore him. The rays of the sun passing through the window give visual form to the popular medieval allegory of the perpetual virginity of Mary, which Saint Bernard explained thus: "Just as the brilliance of the sun fills and penetrates a glass window without damaging it, and pierces its solid form with imperceptible subtlety, neither hurting it when entering nor destroying it when emerging, thus the word of God, the splendor of the Father, entered the virgin chamber and then came forth from the closed womb." Mary's essential humility is shown by the fact that she is seated on the floor instead of on the bench. The mousetraps in Joseph's workshop refer to a sermon of Saint Augustine, who explained that "The cross of the Lord was the devil's mousetrap, the bait by which he was caught was the Lord's death." The Child borne on rays of light through the window in the main scene already carries his cross. The red rose growing on the wall in the donor's garden signifies martyrdom.

The coat of arms on the window at the left has been identified as that of the Ingelbrechts of Malines; the one at the right, with less certainty, as that of the Calcum family. A certain Ingelbrechts is recorded as having had investments in Tournai in 1427, and this may well have been the man in this triptych. When the panel was being cleaned it was discovered that the figure of the woman had been painted over the green grass background; the coats of arms and the sky through the windows in the central panel were also early repaints over the original gold ground. It may be that the donor commissioned the triptych while he was still a bachelor and then ordered these changes made at the time of his marriage.

95. Joseph in his workshop. Detail of the Campin altarpiece

The Campin altarpiece, painted entirely in the new Flemish technique of oil on wood panels, is approximately contemporary with the great Ghent altarpiece by the brothers Van Eyck, which was finished in 1432. The artist, formerly called the Master of the Merode Triptych, then the Master of Flémalle, was identified by Hulin de Loo in 1909 as Robert Campin, master painter of Tournai, who at one time had as apprentices Jacques Daret and the more famous Rogier van der Weyden. This identification is not accepted by all scholars of Flemish painting, but seems convincing to a large number of art historians, including members of the Museum staff. Certainly the known works of Jacques Daret and the early works of Rogier van der Weyden are close in style to works of the master who painted this altarpiece. Campin is mentioned as a master painter in Tournai in 1406; he died in 1444.

MANUSCRIPT PAGES OF THE ANNUNCIATION. In contrast to the Annunciation in the Campin altarpiece, the Annunciation in these two manuscript pages takes place in an ornate churchlike edifice more fantastic than real. The mood is one of make-believe, as if this were an illustration for a fairy tale rather than an interpretation of Christian dogma. The procession of angels who come from heaven to earth, two by two, in a great sweeping arc, is an unusual variation on the theme.

These pages were originally part of the Book of Hours, now in the Bibliothèque Mazarine in Paris, that was made for Charles, duke of Normandy, brother of King Louis XI of France. Evidences of Charles's ownership are two coats of arms—a small one on the angel page and a large one on the verso of the page depicting the Virgin—and an inscription on the border of the latter page that reads: "Charles of France, son of Charles VII, ninth duke of Normandy, in the year 1465. Long may he live."

This Annunciation is related in style to the work of the renowned French painter and illuminator Jean Fouquet of Tours, and has been published as by his hand. Certain differences in drawing, in spatial concepts, and in point of view, however, lead to the conclusion that the pages at The Cloisters were executed by one of several other artists who worked for Charles, duke of Normandy.

PANELS OF THE CRUCIFIXION AND THE LAMENTATION (see fig. 96).

The two brilliantly colored and gilded paintings of the Crucifixion and the Lamentation were painted by a Sienese artist working at the papal court in Avignon, France, about 1340-1350, during the so-called Babylonian Exile, when the French popes transferred their residence to Avignon from Rome. The artist is known as the Master of the Codex of Saint George, having illustrated a manuscript on the life of Saint George (now in the Vatican Archives) for its author, the great art patron Cardinal Stefaneschi.

The panels at The Cloisters suggest the work of a miniaturist, in the jewel-like colors and in the care with which the gilding was applied, so painstaking that scarcely a crack has appeared in six centuries.

The scene of the Crucifixion is treated with restraint. In many Italian paintings of this period, the Virgin is portrayed fainting into the arms of the holy women or Saint John, but here she remains upright, enveloped in a voluminous ultramarine cloak, hugging her grief to herself. Mary Magdalene, often shown clinging despairingly to the foot of the cross, here turns away as if she can scarcely bear to witness the sight. John places his hand on his cheek in a centuries-old, formalized gesture of sorrow.

In the lamentation over the body of Christ, the artist follows closely the description in the *Meditations on the Life of Christ* of Pseudo-Bonaventura. This work by a thirteenth century Franciscan mystic added many imaginative and specific details to the Gospel story; it was so popular that it influenced painters and sculptors for at least two hundred years. The Lamentation, a scene not included

96. *The Lamentation. Painting by the Master of the Codex of Saint George. Italian (Sienese), about 1340–1350*

in the Gospels, is described thus: "Our Lady supports the head and shoulders [of Christ] in her lap, the Magdalen the feet at which she had formerly found so much grace. The others stand about making a great bewailing over him . . . as for a firstborn son." Here, however, the Virgin, who remained upright at the foot of the cross, faints in the arms of one of the holy women.

The artist has been called French by several scholars; it is now generally accepted, however, that although there are certain indications of French influence in these paintings, the Master of the Codex of Saint George was a Sienese painter, summoned to the papal court at Avignon as was his Sienese contemporary Simone Martini.

The two panels at The Cloisters are closely related to two panels in the Bargello in Florence, a *Noli me tangere* and a Coronation of the Virgin; the four paintings may originally have been parts of the same altarpiece. A missal illuminated by this master is one of the treasures of the Pierpont Morgan Library in New York.

THE TAPESTRY with scenes from the life of the Virgin, made of wool, silk, and metal threads on a linen warp, was probably woven in the upper Rhine region in the third quarter of the fifteenth century. Tapestries like this, much smaller in size than contemporary Flemish hangings, were often made by nuns in their convents, not by professional tapestry weavers in large workshops. The scenes represented are the Birth of the Virgin, the Annunciation, the Visitation, the Nativity, the Presentation in the Temple, and the Coronation of the Virgin. All are full of detail, and although done with a certain naïveté they have great charm. The Annunciation repeats almost exactly, though in reverse, the composition of a small painting, attributed to an upper Rhenish master, in the collection of Oskar Rheinhart in Winterthur, Switzerland. The tapestry was undoubtedly woven to be used as an altar frontal.

THE LATE GOTHIC HALL

From the standpoint of architecture the Late Gothic Hall (fig. 97) may be considered the refectory of The Cloisters. Its timbered ceiling, made with hand-worked beams taken from old Connecticut buildings, is in the style of some late medieval examples. The fifteenth century windows are four of the six which were originally in the refectory of the convent of the Dominicans at Sens. All the windows were probably glazed, and convent records show that in the sixteenth century at least one was filled with stained and painted glass. Three of the four late medieval limestone doorways are unusually fine and well preserved. In the late Middle Ages, as in the late stages of other periods, there was a tendency to exaggerate and make stilted the earlier vocabulary. Although complicated moldings and details are emphasized, these doorways are structurally logical in their ornamentation as well as their form.

RETABLES, or altarpieces, brought together in this hall are unusual examples of Spanish painting. Such works rivaled in splendor the lavish tombs of the later Middle Ages. From the fourteenth century through the late medieval period and the Renaissance, retables became more numerous and larger. They rose impressively, high above the main altars, and were also used in subordinate chapels. Unlike portable shrines, they were architectural ensembles related to the space around them. Generally Spanish retables were higher than they were broad, and were not provided with folding wings. Like great billboards, they had a story to tell, and the bigger their proportions, the more easily the scenes could be read. The usual arrangement included a large central panel and numerous smaller ones depicting scenes related to the principal subject. Ordi-

194

97. The Late Gothic Hall

narily the predella, or bottom member of the retable, illustrated other anecdotes. The scenes were colorful, realistic, and elaborated in great detail. In the fourteenth century Spanish painting was influenced by the Sienese and other Italian schools; in the fifteenth century Flemish influences predominated.

THE SAINT ANDREW RETABLE is an important example of Catalan painting of the first quarter of the fifteenth century, close in style to the work of Luis Borrassá. It is painted in tempera on wood panels, and conventionalized oak leaves enrich the framework. The central panel with Saint Andrew enthroned is surmounted by a panel with the Virgin and Child, Saint Catherine, Saint Mary Magdalene, and angels. At the left are panels depicting the calling of Saint Andrew and the punishment of a wicked mother, who was killed by fire from heaven in Saint Andrew's presence. At the right are the crucifixion of Saint Andrew and Saint Andrew saving a bishop from the devil disguised as a fair woman. In the predella are shown, from left to right, Saint Andrew and the woman who prayed to Diana on behalf of her sister; the woman bringing the saint to her sister; Saint Andrew driving away devils that had taken the form of dogs; the Man of Sorrows; Saint Andrew raising a dead youth; and Saint Andrew bringing to life drowned men.

THE SAINT JOHN THE BAPTIST RETABLE is made up of separate panels which have been cleaned and put together to form a retable such as they must once have composed. No attempt has been made to reconstruct the carved and gilded canopies that would originally have been placed over the individual scenes, and only simple moldings, consistent with old molding on the predella, have been used for the framework. A Crucifixion scene, with the swooning Virgin supported by Saint John and two holy women, and with four men casting lots for the seamless garment of Christ, surmounts the entire composition. The large central panel represents Saint John seated on a throne; in his raised left hand he holds his attribute, the book with the Lamb of God upon it. The smaller panels, beginning in the upper left-hand corner and continuing in each register from left to right, depict the following scenes in the saint's life: the angel appearing to Zacharias, the father of John the Baptist; the Visitation of the Virgin Mary to Elisabeth; the birth of John the Baptist; his preaching beside the Jordan; his baptism of Christ; his reproof of Herod; his beheading and the presentation of his head to Herodias.

The predella consists of two parts, each composed of three panels with paintings of saints. Carved and gilded arcading above and crocketed columns at the sides frame the individual panels in such a way as to create niches for the saints. A central panel now used for the label was originally intended either for another painting or more probably for a small carved and gilded wood tabernacle in which the Host was kept. The panels, from left to right, represent Saint Martial (inscribed *Sant Marcal*), Saint Sebastian (*Sant Sabastia*), Saint Mary Magdalene (*Santa Mag*), Saint Bridget (*Santa Brigida*), Saint Christopher carrying the Christ child (without inscription), and Saint Kilian (*Sant Quilez*).

In all the compositions the figures predominate, the architecture and the landscape of the backgrounds being secondary. The expressiveness of the faces contrasts sharply with the woodenness of the figures, which are garbed in almost schematic late Gothic draperies. The costumes are painted in gay, lively colors. Crimson and vermilion, grass green, white, and patches of yellow stand out among the softer tones of olive drab, purple, deep blue, and a variety of other shades. Several of the garments, especially those of Zacharias, and the bed coverlet in the scene of the birth of Saint John are richly patterned in gold, as are other details. In striking contrast is the ascetic costume of Saint John. Tones of gray are employed chiefly for the buildings, against which the bright figures are silhouetted. Certain details are stressed by the juxtaposition of contrasting colors, as for instance in the Baptism, where God the Father with his gold halo is looking down from a yellow orb surrounded by concentric bands of red and blue.

The central panel of the retable of Saint John the Baptist is like the incomplete retable with three large panels representing Saint Isidore, Saint Ambrose, and Saint Nicholas, in the collegiate church of Santa María de Calatayud in the province of Saragossa, and has an almost identical predella. Both, however, must be compared to the great retable in the chapel of the Piedad at San Llorens dels Morunys, which according to accepted documents was "painted" on July 17, 1480 by Francisco Solibes de Bañolas. In all probability all three retables were painted by this master, a Catalan who may have worked in Aragon.

THE RETABLE OF SAINT ANNE with the Virgin and Child (see fig. 97) is over fifteen feet high. Saint Anne is seated on an elaborate Gothic throne on which there are niches with Adam and Eve and figures, probably angels, with musical instruments. In the panel above is the Crucifixion, with Christ and the two thieves, the Virgin, the three Marys, and Saint John the Evangelist. At the left are the Virgin of the Rosary, standing in a mandorla of flames, with four angels playing musical instruments; and, above, the miracle in which, according to legend, a gentleman of Cologne who had killed a friend in a quarrel was saved from the vengeance of the victim's brother by the Virgin, who placed a garland of roses on his head as he kneeled before her altar. At the right are Saint Michael weighing two souls and trampling a demon symbolizing Satan, and, above, Saint Michael's miracle at Monte Gargano. In this version Dominican monks followed by a pope, two cardinals, bishops, nobles, and ladies lead the way to the cave where a bull indicates the site for a church. The predella shows Joachim and Anne expelled from the temple; their meeting at the Golden Gate; the Mass of Saint Gregory; the Birth of the Virgin; and her Presentation in the Temple. On the dust guards (*guardapolvos*) are angels bearing instruments of the Passion.

This retable, from a monastery at Teruel, was painted in the second half of the fifteenth century. The original text of the inscription may be read as follows: . . . *An fecho fazer los muy onrados Mosén Miguel Armisén i Atón Incet en el anyo de mi*[*l*] CCCC-[LXXXIII] (The most honorable Mosén Miguel Armisén and Atón Incet have caused [it] to be made in the year 14[83]). Unfortunately the raised gold letters at the two ends have been restored, and the date is therefore uncertain.

98. The Three Kings. German, about 1489

THE THREE KINGS (fig. 98), life-size figures of Caspar, Balthasar, and Melchior, were carved about 1490 as part of the retable of the high altar of the convent of Lichtenthal in Baden, Germany. The Virgin and Child from the group remains at the convent. The painted wings of the retable, for many years in Mannheim, were recently exhibited in Karlsruhe.

These three kings are especially appealing in the vivacity of their poses. The movement of each statue is self-contained when considered alone but becomes part of a dramatic whole when the group is assembled. The statues recall the work of the Ulm sculptor Jörg Syrlin the Younger, and the morris dancers by Erasmus Grasser in the old city hall in Munich. A stained glass window in one of the painted panels of the altarpiece bears the arms of Baden in the center, surrounded by a German inscription stating that the window was given by Lady "Margret," who was born a margravine and became the abbess of Lichtenthal in the year 1489. The altarpiece was probably executed about that time and in no event after Margaretha's death in 1496.

According to the records, in 1757 a painting was substituted for the sculptures of the altarpiece because they were damaged. When the three kings were auctioned in London in 1939, they had been repainted and refurbished with baroque garments. The purchaser removed many of these additions and the Museum later completed the restoration. The remaining paint on the middle king, Balthasar, is in a remarkable state of preservation.

THE KNEELING VIRGIN (fig. 99) from a Nativity group, an early sixteenth century sculpture, continues the tradition of central Italian medieval wood carving. Strictly speaking, this is a Renaissance work, but as it has long been at The Cloisters and is reminiscent of earlier wood carving it is exhibited here. It is related to a group of wood sculptures, including a Virgin at Chieti, a Virgin and Child at Teramo, and similar groups in the Museo

99. The Virgin kneeling. Italian, early XVI *century*

Civico at Aquila. It is attributed to Gagliardelli, of whom little is known except that he lived at Città Sant' Angelo and at Chieti and practiced painting as well as sculpture. He contracted to do a group of the Virgin and Child for Santa Maria Magna in Ripatransone in 1524 and painted a fresco for the same church in 1526.

THE STATUE OF SAINT ROCH in painted wood, also a sixteenth century work, is said to have come from Cherbourg. There are many stories told about the saint. One concerns an incident alleged to have taken place when the Council of Constance was about to be adjourned in 1414, owing to the plague. According to tradition, the plague came to an end when, at the suggestion of a young German monk who had traveled in France and there had heard wondrous tales of Saint Roch, the council ordered an effigy of the saint to be carried in a procession through the streets.

THE STATUE OF SAINT MICHAEL, in wood, displayed on a corbel on the north wall of the gallery, follows a type prevalent in Spanish painting of the fifteenth and sixteenth centuries. Clad in armor intricately carved and polychromed, and wearing a long, full cloak, the saint treads upon the devil depicted as a winged dragon. The right hand no doubt once held the lance and the left carried the scales, symbolic of the Last Judgment of human souls. The style, properly Hispano-Flemish in character, compares to works executed in the region around Burgos. The sculpture dates in the first decade of the sixteenth century.

THE PASCHAL CANDLESTICK. A special very large candlestick was required in the Middle Ages, as today, for the celebration of the Easter festival. On Easter Eve a large paschal candle, placed in the candlestick, was solemnly blessed and ceremoniously lighted from newly kindled fire to symbolize the glory of Christ's resurrection. The candle was afterward relighted for all services of the Church for at least the forty days between Easter and the Feast of the Ascension. Easter candlesticks were sometimes of wax like the candles, sometimes of bronze or precious metals, sometimes of wood or stone. The Cloisters candlestick is of wood, painted and gilded; it is six feet five inches in height and is in the form of a hexagonal shaft tapering at the top. Against backgrounds of tooled gold are three bands of figures painted in tones of leaf green, salmon, olive gray, and vermilion. In the upper tier are six personages of the Old Law, in the middle tier six saints, and in the bottom register six apostles. These paintings have been related to the work of Jorge Inglés, who painted the Retable of the Angels for the chapel of the hospital at Buitrago, south of Burgos, in the second half of the fifteenth century.

THE FROVILLE ARCADE

The exterior of the entrance passageway along the upper driveway is formed by nine pointed, cusped arches from the fifteenth century cloister of the Benedictine priory of Froville (fig. 100). The arches are placed on a parapet in groups of three and separated by buttresses, as they were at Froville.

Arcades of this type were frequently employed in fourteenth and fifteenth century cloisters, for they permitted solid construction and did not require great ingenuity of the artist or particular skill of the stonecutter, as did the more elaborately carved Romanesque and early Gothic arcades. By the end of the Middle Ages arcades were in most instances treated as a series of windows. In the Renaissance and later periods cloisters derived their impressiveness from their proportions rather than from the decoration of the architecture.

The original cloister at Froville was located on the north side of the church, near the tower. It had a small, square court with nine arches on each side. Over the cloister walk there was a second story, a stringcourse above the arches indicating the floor level. The rubble walls were originally plastered, and it is possible that even the stone arches were covered. It has been suggested that the toolmarks were left on the surface of the stone so that the plaster would adhere.

A document of the year 1091 records that a nobleman named Odouin gave the church and other properties to the Benedictine abbey of Cluny, and thus the priory of Froville was founded. The priory suffered during the Thirty Years' War (1618–1648). In 1791 it was confiscated and sold by the state and the property was used as a farm. One side of the cloister was still standing in 1920; the other sides had been demolished before 1904 to make room for the building of stables.

204

100. A view of The Cloisters showing windows from Sens and the Froville Arcade

INDEX

This index is confined mainly to objects in the Cloisters collection and to the names of persons and places related to them. Objects are listed by provenance and under such categories as Architecture, Metalwork, Paintings, Sculpture. Illustration references are in italics.

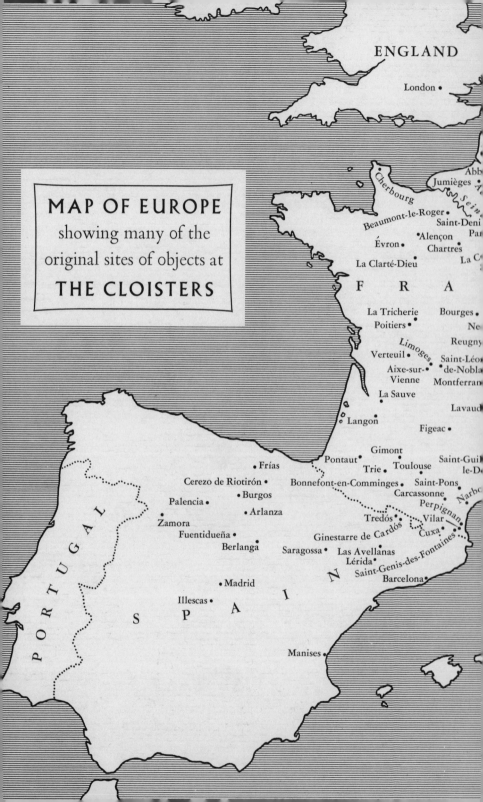

ENGLAND

London •

Cherbourg

Abb

Jumièges •

Seine

Beaumont-le-Roger •

Saint-Deni

•Alençon   Par

Évron •   Chartres

La Clarté-Dieu   La C

F   R   A

La Tricherie   Bourges •

Poitiers •   Ne

Reugny

Limoges

Verteuil •   Saint-Léo

Aixe-sur- •   de-Nobla

Vienne   Montferran

La Sauve

Lavaud

Langon •

Figeac •

Gimont

• Frías   Pontaut •   Trie • Toulouse   Saint-Gui

le-D

Cerezo de Riotirón •   Bonnefont-en-Comminges •   Saint-Pons

• Burgos   Carcassonne

Palencia •   Perpignan

• Arlanza   Tredós •   Vilar   Narbo

Zamora •   Ginestarre de Cardós   Cuxa

Fuentidueña •   Saragossa •   Las Avellanas

Berlanga •   Lérida •

Saint-Genis-des-Fontaines

Barcelona •

• Madrid

Illescas •

S   A   I   N

Manises •

MAP OF EUROPE
showing many of the
original sites of objects at
THE CLOISTERS

PORTUGAL

S   P   A   I